ABC TO CEO

The Ambitious Young Woman's Guide to Becoming the Boss

SHARON FIEHLER

ABC to CEO™

ABC TO CEO
The Ambitious Young Woman's Guide to Becoming the Boss

FIRST EDITION

Published by ABC To CEO

ISBN   979-8-9918072-0-3   *Hardcover*
        979-8-9918072-1-0   *Paperback*
        979-8-9918072-2-7   *eBook*

Cover and interior design by Jason Arias

For more information about the book or to contact the author, visit www.abctoceo.org/book

*This book is dedicated to all women who are willing
to reach outside of their comfort zone.*

TABLE OF CONTENTS

CEO
INSIGHT

"It is better to look ahead and prepare than to look back and regret."

———

—Jackie Joyner-Kersee, *A Kind of Grace*

Chapter 1

WHAT YOU DON'T KNOW ABOUT BECOMING A CEO

AND WHAT YOU NEED TO KNOW *NOW* TO PREPARE FOR THE POSSIBILITY

H ey there, future game changer! Are you ready to embark on a journey unlike any other? One that redefines the leadership roadmap for young women everywhere? In the pages that follow, we'll explore what it means to aspire, achieve, and lead with a purpose that resonates beyond what you might imagine today.

It's about reimagining what the corporate ladder looks like for women in their twenties and beyond, making the role of chief executive officer (CEO) not just a distant dream but a tangible goal.

Have you ever thought about becoming a CEO? If not, you aren't alone. For most women, the possibility never crosses their radar.

I'm here to tell you that you *can* become a CEO. It *is* a possibility! One of my favorite quotes from George Bernard Shaw encapsulates our mission here:

"Life isn't about finding yourself. Life is about creating yourself."

That's precisely the mindset I embraced. I didn't stumble upon success in my career; I built it, piece by piece, through my strong work ethic and by earning the trust of leaders around me. With this book, I'll guide you as you create the person you're capable of becoming.

I had a long and successful career in my last role as a C-suite executive at a Fortune 500 Company. (Note: The term "C-suite" refers to a company's executive-level, or "chief", managers, such as the chief operating officer, chief financial officer, and chief administrative officer. The head of this group is the CEO.) While there's no such thing as "retiring" in my Book of Life, before I became "post-career" in 2014, I managed a portfolio of global, multidepartmental functions and a $250 million operating budget. I worked directly under several CEOs who provided me with many growth opportunities. During that time, I also chaired the board of the 8th District of the US Federal Reserve.

In spite of all my success, however, you might have noticed something was missing: I never sat in the CEO chair. One reason is because I never thought about it, nor was a seed ever planted for me to consider it. As a result, I lacked the fundamental experience to become a successful CEO, such as line and commercial roles—operations, product development, and sales—and, most importantly, profit and loss (P&L) roles. If you take anything away from this book, I want you to remember this:

Most women don't lack the talent to become CEO; they lack the *right experiences*.

Don't miss the operative words there: the right experiences. Pay attention! I'll be referencing this critical point numerous times throughout this book.

Although I had a wonderful career as a C-suite executive, continually taking on more staff responsibilities instead of line roles didn't prepare me for becoming a CEO. I oversaw important global functions—information technology (IT), human resources (HR), supply chain management, and security to name a few—but they were back-office staff roles that didn't give me the credentials for the CEO position.

Looking back, I never considered becoming a CEO, nor did I understand which roles would prepare me for that position. However, other pioneering women learned early on in their careers which path to take and made it to CEO over a decade ago, when publicly traded companies had very few women in this role. Here are some of these early trail-blazers: Virginia Rometty, Ursula Burns, Margaret Whitman, Indra Nooyi, Marissa Mayer, Diane Sullivan, Kathleen Mazzarella, Kim Popovits, and Pamela Nichols to name a few. My hat goes off to them for envisioning what I and many other women didn't.

I would have embraced the challenge, but it would have required a different career strategy and a different vision, one with intentionality and proper preparation. At the time, I didn't know it was possible for someone like me to be the CEO. I wish I'd had the foresight to envision this for myself. Or I wish someone had planted a seed for me and shown me what I needed to do to get there.

So I'm writing this book to tell you that you can become a CEO. I want to plant the seed for you and share how you can carve your path, create your own success, and, ultimately, take a seat at the head of the table.

WHY ABC TO CEO?

I founded ABC to CEO to inspire and prepare the next generation of women leaders. My goal is to enable more women to reach top leadership positions and become CEOs. With numerous podcast interviews with CEOs and other leaders, inspiring social media content, online education materials, and a website packed with leadership tips, ABC to CEO helps young women like you navigate the maze of career opportunities and see that with desire, proper preparation, and a track record of stellar performance, reaching the top is possible.

I've spent over thirty-five years working with and observing leaders, including overseeing talent management teams. This experience has given me insight into how individuals are evaluated for upward movement and promotion. I've seen talented employees stall in their advancement while less talented ones excel, and I can recognize the signs of who is likely to rise to senior leadership.

My perspective in this book is based on my experience on the executive leadership team of a multibillion-dollar publicly traded corporation, and, although a lot of the information discussed in this book is applicable to leadership in general, much of the advice is geared toward large organizations.

Young, ambitious women are often overlooked for entry-level roles that pave the way to executive leadership and CEO positions. This isn't because young women lack the talent or drive, but because historically, women have been placed in support roles, while men hold the line and commercial roles. This disparity occurs long before young women reach the midpoint of their career. I believe this is the root cause of why fewer women than men become qualified for the CEO role. It's time to change that.

As I write this in 2025, public awareness is growing around the fact that women still make up less than 10 percent of CEOs in publicly traded companies. The conversation is shifting toward identifying the primary barriers holding women like you back and finding ways to better support and prepare you to take on these top roles. That's why this book is important.

Despite the progress in recent years with more women making it to the C-suite, the current statistics make it clear that there's still much more work to be done to make women as qualified as men to become CEOs. A 2023 study by Russell Reynolds (an international executive search and leadership advisory firm) stated that based on the current number of women in CEO positions, gender equality in C-suite roles won't arrive for almost another *century*. You read that right! *Not another decade—another century!*[1]

Outdated assumptions and biases about women's abilities and ambitions still persist. Changing this narrative requires a concerted effort to challenge these perceptions and give women the right experiences so they can make it to the top, particularly in the traditionally male-dominated roles of operations, product development, and sales. Senior decision-makers in the talent management arena must revisit how they develop women within their organizations. And young women like you need to pursue roles outside of support roles, which means you need to actively manage your career and stop allowing other people to manage you.

Additionally, we all must continue to spotlight success stories of female CEOs to create more visible role models for young women. Companies (and women themselves) need to know which promotions lead to becoming a CEO and which lead to career dead ends.

The narrative will keep evolving as more and more women ascend to CEO positions. As Billie Jean King said, "And if you can see it, you can be it." [2] After reading this book, you'll be able to see it, too.

HIGH-LEVEL INSIGHTS, PRACTICAL GUIDANCE, AND TOOLS

This book is the ABC's of starting you on your path to the CEO chair. It gives you the fundamentals you need to know as you begin your professional journey. It will offer you a mix of high-level insights and inspiration, along with practical guidance and tools. Here's what this book will give you:

- Advice and lessons learned from current and former CEOs (as featured in ABC to CEO's podcast, Preparing for the Possibility)
- Suggestions to help you build the confidence and skills needed to pursue leadership roles
- Guidance on mapping out your career path, including explanations for the types of roles available and which experiences to pursue and which to avoid getting stuck in
- Tips for building a strong professional network of mentors, supporters, and promoters
- Insights on how to stand out as a leader and position yourself for the right promotional opportunities

I'll also include advice that you can translate into actionable plans for your career. My goal is to give you a comprehensive resource for owning your ambition, kick-starting your leadership development, charting your career journey to CEO, and avoiding roadblocks.

IF I HAD ENVISIONED IT SOONER . . .

When I reflect on my career, one thought lingers: if only I had considered the possibility of becoming a CEO early in my career. Like many women of my generation, I began my professional journey without any thought of becoming a CEO. Leadership came naturally to me from an early age (yes, I was called "bossy"), but the idea of aiming for the top of my company never crossed my mind. Instead, I focused on immediate success, gaining promotions and proving myself in every role I took on. What I didn't realize was that these achievements, while fulfilling, were sometimes leading me further away from the role of CEO. I was moving up—but not on the right path. I didn't think to look beyond the next promotion to see that leadership at the highest level was not just a possibility but a path I could choose.

This book is born out of that realization—out of the desire to give young women like you the vision I never had, to help you see the bigger picture earlier in your careers. I continue to admire the women of my generation, and the generations before me, who made it to CEO on their own with little guidance and even fewer female CEO role models; they were quite special in many ways.

This book is for you as a young woman who has the potential to lead but may not yet envision yourself as a CEO. It's easy to focus on immediate success and miss the broader opportunity to steer your career toward leadership. Society often doesn't encourage young women to become CEOs; we're taught to excel but not always to aim for the very top. I want to change that. Whether you're just starting your career or are already climbing the ladder, it's important to recognize that the skills, ambition, and leadership qualities you already possess can propel you to the highest levels of your organization. But only if you know the right moves to make. This book is for every young woman who feels the spark of leadership but hasn't yet been shown how to nurture it into a flame that can light her path to the top.

In writing this book, I want to plant the seed of possibility in your mind. If you're anything like I was, you're ambitious, you work hard, you take pride in doing a great job, and you know you have the potential to achieve great things. Kim Popovits—a successful CEO who led Genomic Health, a company that revolutionized breast cancer diagnosis and treatment—once described herself to me as "an ordinary person who has been able to do extraordinary things." So if you think "ordinary" people can't move mountains, think again!

But potential needs direction. The road to becoming a CEO isn't a straightforward climb; it's a series of decisions and mindsets, many of which need to be made early on. I want to guide you on the right steps to take, the signs to look for, and the paths to avoid. I'll discuss the traits of a successful CEO and the people to seek advice from along the way. That's what this book will give you—a clearer view of how to navigate your career strategically.

I'll also share the common missteps women make, not because they lack talent or drive, but because they're simply unaware of the nuances of the CEO path—a path that is often clearer to young men since they have other men's footsteps to follow. My hope is that this awareness will help you avoid unnecessary detours and lost time and, instead, equip you with the tools to stay on course toward the top. Of course, in the end, it's all about your performance in the roles you take on. Having an exceptional track record for executing your goals is critical.

This book is not a one-size-fits-all guide to becoming a CEO because the truth is there isn't just one path to the top. There are multiple ways to build a career, but there are also many wrong turns that can keep you from reaching your destination. I've seen many talented women strive to reach the top and accept roles that seemed like the right next step, only to find themselves stuck at a dead end. I'll help you recognize those turning points, where the right move can keep you on track and the wrong one can derail your ambitions. It's about understanding the landscape of your career and knowing which paths will lead you forward and which ones will distract you from your potential.

In these pages, you'll learn not only what it takes to become a CEO but why that role might be the right one for you. For some women, the idea of becoming a CEO not only seems unrealistic, something reserved for others, but also may not be enticing. I want to challenge that perception. Becoming a CEO isn't just about gaining power or prestige; it's about having the influence to shape your company, your industry, and even society. It's about giving people a product or service to make their lives better. It's about leading a team to build something that reflects your vision and values. This book will help you see why becoming a CEO can be one of the most fulfilling and impactful goals you can strive for—and how you can structure your career to make it a possibility.

This book is your invitation to dream big, to position yourself for success, to break free from the expectations that limit your career ambitions, and to consider a future where you aren't just a part of the team but the leader. It's a roadmap for making bold decisions, for owning your career, and for recognizing your potential to be more than you ever thought possible. My journey was limited because I never considered becoming a CEO, but yours doesn't have to be. With this book in hand, you can forge a path toward leadership with confidence, clarity, and the understanding that the top isn't out of reach—it's waiting for you.

So let's get started, future CEO! It's time for you to climb into the driver's seat and begin your exciting journey!

ABC CALLOUTS

Let's break down the ABC's of preparing for a future as a CEO:

A. Acknowledge the path to CEO: Many women don't reach the CEO chair not due to lack of talent but because they lack the right experiences. Recognize early on that line roles in operations, sales, and product development are essential to your preparation. Identify the skills and experiences you need now to avoid dead-end roles later.

B. Build a strategic vision: Success doesn't just happen—it's created. As George Bernard Shaw said, "Life isn't about finding yourself. Life is about creating yourself." Take control of your career trajectory by setting a clear vision, embracing intentionality, and mapping your path to leadership. Start thinking about where you want to be and plan accordingly.

C. Cultivate CEO skills: The traits of a successful CEO—visionary thinking, bold decision-making, and emotional intelligence—don't develop overnight. Seek out opportunities to stretch yourself. Focus on leadership roles that test your ability to manage P&L, innovate solutions, and rally teams around a common goal. Remember: It's not just about working hard—it's about working smart and preparing yourself for the top.

CEO
INSIGHT

*"Nothing in life is to be feared;
it is only to be understood. Now is the time to
understand more so that we may fear less."*

———

—Marie Curie, the first woman to win a Nobel Prize

Chapter 2

WHY WOULD YOU WANT TO BE A CEO?

LET'S THINK ABOUT BECOMING AN INFLUENCER ...A MAJOR INFLUENCER!

L et's tackle the BIG question up front: Why should you set your sights on becoming a CEO?

It sounds like a lofty goal, and you may even be a bit intimidated. But hear me out.

Aiming for that CEO chair is about way more than nabbing that corner office or the seat at the head of the table.

It's about impact. Major impact.

We're talking about shaping whole industries and technologies, and maybe even making a bit of history in the process. The CEO role is all about transforming visions into reality, sparking innovation, and building a culture that rocks. It's about providing something, whether it's a product or service, that improves the lives of others.

From the CEO chair, *you can make changes that might impact the world!*

You can change lives, even millions of lives, for the better!

You can change entire communities!

You can influence public policy!

Look around you, almost everything you touch and experience comes from a company that was led by a CEO—from cell phones to computers, from medical advances to medical equipment, from self-driving cars to drones. The list goes on and on.

You're probably asking, "How can a CEO do all of this?" Of course, they don't do it alone. They are the visionaries who lead teams . . . teams of people who take ideas and make them a reality.

As a successful CEO, you can influence and guide an organization's

- mission and strategic direction,
- overall culture,
- customer relationships,
- investor and stakeholder engagement, and
- products and services.

But that's not all!

Leadership at this level allows you to shape a company's destiny, influence its culture, and make a lasting impact on the world. It's about leading a team toward a vision that maybe only you can see clearly at the beginning.

You've probably already been a leader at some level. Maybe in high school or college, maybe in sports, maybe in community events, maybe in nonprofit organizations. If so, you're already prepared to take the next path. In the end, the choice of how far you want to take your leadership skills is up to you.

I hope that this book gives you the knowledge you need to realize your fullest potential, whether it's a CEO or another type of leader. Remember, every leader started their career somewhere. Yours is beginning now! Great opportunities await you, and *now* is the time to find them.

PLANT YOUR CEO SEEDS EARLY

Let's take a moment to zoom out and see the bigger picture. Leadership seeds can be sown early and in the most unexpected soils, but for many, the path to CEO begins after their career has already taken shape and bold choices have been made.

The conclusion we're drawing here? Your leadership journey isn't a distant dream or a path reserved for a chosen few. It begins with recognizing and harnessing the power of influences in your life. It grows by taking risks, pushing beyond your comfort zone, and reaching for goals that others might deem too lofty.

Your journey to leadership—and to becoming the CEO—can start now.

I once did an episode of *Preparing for the Possibility* with Luann Abrams, the founder of CEOX, an organization that connects female candidates to CEO roles. We discussed why fewer women than men consider becoming a CEO, and Luann shared an interesting observation from her discussions with existing female CEOs:

"One thing that stands out is how many never considered being a CEO early on in their careers. And it was only as they got older, it started to become something that they thought of. And pretty much all of them said if it had been something they had thought of earlier, it probably would have happened earlier." [3]

So even for women who made it to CEO, some believe they were late to the game because they didn't consider it at an earlier age.

Embrace the possibility of becoming a CEO with the same courage and determination that you'll find in the lessons and stories in this book. Believe in your potential to lead, innovate, and inspire. Your leadership potential exists, waiting to be unlocked with determination, a clear vision, and an unwavering belief in your capabilities.

In the next chapter, you'll hear many similar themes in slightly different ways. So as you delve into these materials, I'll be repeating some concepts on purpose to help you better retain them.

Are you ready? Because the world is waiting for leaders just like you.

DEVELOP A CEO MINDSET

Alright, let's dive into the nitty-gritty of what it takes to develop a true CEO mindset. This isn't just about thinking positive thoughts or visualizing success—it's about fundamentally shifting the way you approach your career and your leadership.

At its core, the CEO mindset is all about translating visionary thinking into action. It's about having the courage to dream big, set audacious goals, and then take the bold steps needed to make those dreams a reality. It's about being willing to take risks and make tough calls in the face of uncertainty and adversity. It's about seeing a future different from what exists today.

But developing a CEO mindset isn't just about grand visions and bold moves. It's also about cultivating the day-to-day habits and attitudes that define successful leaders.

What does this mean for you today?

It means developing resilience in the face of setbacks, maintaining strategic focus in chaos, and always keeping your goals and impact in mind. It also means never having a "victim" mentality. Even when things happen that may be beyond your control, you need to overcome it and move forward. If there's a lesson to learn, take note and find another path forward. You need a winner's mindset.

One of the key thought patterns of successful CEOs is the ability to see opportunity where others only see obstacles. This means having the mental flexibility to pivot when necessary, the creativity to find innovative solutions to complex problems, and the optimism to believe that even the most daunting challenges can be overcome. You can practice these mindsets in your current role. The next time you're faced with a problem, consider a pivot. Be innovative and stay optimistic.

Another critical attitude that defines the CEO mindset is a relentless drive for excellence. This means setting the bar high for yourself and your team, continuously pushing to improve and innovate, and never settling for "good enough." It means holding yourself and others accountable to the highest standards of performance and integrity and always striving for the top of your field.

Developing a CEO mindset isn't something that happens overnight. It's a process of continuous growth and self-reflection. You need to constantly challenge your assumptions, seek out new perspectives and experiences, and push yourself outside of your comfort zone.

On an episode of *Preparing for the Possibility*, I interviewed DeLisa Guerrier—a managing partner at Guerrier Development, one of the largest real estate and investments development companies in Nashville, Tennessee. She stated:

> "We can think as big as we want; we can go after something small or something big, and that thought or that scale really sets our path." [4]

Now is the time to set your sights on something BIG!

The payoff of cultivating a CEO mindset is immense. When you approach your career with the vision, decisiveness, and resilience of a true leader, you'll unlock your full potential and set yourself on a trajectory that leads to greater opportunities.

So start shifting your thinking, future CEO. Take off! Embrace the challenges, take bold action, and never stop growing and evolving. Your path starts with your mindset, so make it a great one.

MASTER KEY LEADERSHIP SKILLS

Alright, future CEO, you've got the mindset nailed down. Now it's time to focus on the key leadership skills that'll move you upward. These aren't just nice-to-haves; they're the essential tools in your CEO toolkit, the skills that'll set you apart from the rest and help you navigate even the toughest challenges.

COMMUNICATION AND "WALKING THE TALK"

As a CEO, your words carry weight. They can inspire, motivate, and spur your team to action. Your team will look to you as a role model for embodying your beliefs. But great communication isn't just about giving a killer speech or writing a compelling email; it's about doing and listening. The best CEOs are active-listening masters, able to truly hear and understand their team members', customers', and stakeholders' perspectives. They know that great ideas can come from anywhere, and they create an environment where everyone feels heard and valued.

On an episode of *Preparing for the Possibility*, I interviewed Jenny Bristow, the CEO and founder of Hedy & Hopp, a health-care marketing agency. She had this to say about communicating as her company's CEO:

> "We found that the more information we shared with our employees, the better stewards they can be for making our business more successful." [5]

As you begin your career and start managing teams, this is great advice to remember. Effective communication is invaluable.

Start enhancing your communication skills now. Improve your written skills by taking classes with a communications expert, online or in person. As you move up the ladder of success, you'll likely have someone writing your communications for you, but getting comfortable with it now will pay off in the future. Public speaking, however . . . now that's another game altogether. It's all about you and your delivery. Find a professional coach to help you develop your public speaking presence; you'll never regret becoming a good speaker. The earlier you begin enhancing these skills, the more natural they'll become in the future. And remember, always walk the talk. Being authentic will show others that they can trust you, a critical trait of a good leader that we'll talk more about later.

My late friend and mentor, Dr. Kathy Cramer, the CEO and founder of The Cramer Institute, always included the phrase "substance, sizzle, and soul" in her writings and speeches. That's one of many life-long lessons I learned from her, and now I'm passing it onto you as an effective tip for your communications, too.

DECISION-MAKING

CEOs are faced with tough calls every day, from strategic pivots to resource allocations to personnel management. The key to great decision-making is having a clear, data-driven process in place. This means gathering all the relevant information, seeking out diverse perspectives, and weighing the pros and cons of each option. But it also means trusting your judgment, knowing when to follow your instincts despite the data, and making bold moves, even in the face of uncertainty.

EMOTIONAL INTELLIGENCE

Also known as your emotional quotient (EQ), emotional intelligence is being aware of your own emotions and being attentive to others'. CEOs with high EQ build strong, trusting relationships with their teams, respect their team members regardless of rank, and create a culture of openness and collaboration. They're good listeners, know how to "read a room," can navigate complex interpersonal dynamics, and inspire others to bring their best selves to work every day. They're attuned to observing other people's behaviors and understanding where they're coming from. We've probably all met leaders who succeeded without a lot of EQ, and it always makes me wonder how much better at leading they would have been with more EQ.

In the early stages of your career, looking for these traits is one way to learn them. Seek out leaders with high EQs, identify what makes them different, and learn to develop these traits yourself.

Start by understanding your own EQ by asking colleagues for feedback. Sometimes hearing what isn't working for you is the most valuable feedback. Developmental training organizations also offer tests that can help you. Be proactive in learning these traits; they may not always come naturally, but over time, most of us can become better at them.

THEN ... CULTIVATE THEM

Cultivating your leadership skills is an ongoing process—one that requires a commitment to lifelong learning and a willingness to step outside your comfort zone. Whether you're just starting out on your leadership journey or you're a seasoned executive, there are always new ways to stretch yourself and expand your capabilities.

There are multiple ways to cultivate your leadership skills. One way is through formal learning opportunities, for example, pursuing an advanced degree such as an MBA or another type of executive education course. These programs can teach you key business concepts, expose you to new ideas and perspectives, and give you the opportunity to network with other leaders from diverse backgrounds and industries. An advanced degree or certification opens another avenue for you to differentiate yourself from other candidates.

But formal learning is just one piece of the puzzle. Informal learning opportunities from everyday experiences and interactions are just as important, if not more so! Seek out mentors who can provide guidance and support, take on stretch assignments that push you beyond your current skill set, or simply ask for feedback and constructive criticism from colleagues and team members.

Another opportunity to cultivate your leadership skills is when you're faced with complex problems. Great leaders maintain their cool during times of chaos. If you've ever been there, you know the difference between a leader who remains focused under stress and those who lose it. Teams lose confidence when they think their leaders can't lead them through a storm. No matter what stage of your career you're in, sometimes the unexpected happens. It's easy to let your emotions control you when it does, but this is where you need to begin practicing staying calm and focused. Your team will pick up on it. I've been on teams with both kinds of leaders and can attest that the team always watches the leader's behavior in stressful situations. A confident leader will inspire their team, who will in turn perform with confidence.

Cultivating your leadership skills also means being self-aware and intentional in your personal growth. This might involve reflecting on your strengths and weaknesses, setting goals for your personal development, and seeking out opportunities to practice new skills and behaviors. It might also mean taking risks and stepping outside your comfort zone—whether that means speaking up in a meeting, taking on a new project, or advocating for a bold new idea.

Ultimately, cultivating your leadership skills is about embracing a growth mindset—a belief that you can develop your abilities and talents through hard work, dedication, and a willingness to learn. By approaching your leadership journey with curiosity and a commitment to ongoing growth and development, you'll be well-equipped to tackle whatever challenges come your way while inspiring and empowering others to do the same.

LEAD WITH PURPOSE

Leadership, in all its forms, is a noble pursuit. Yet, if you're angling to become a CEO, the journey demands *more* than just leadership ability. It's about infusing your leadership with *intention*, vision, and a strategy that resonates with your deepest values. It's about transforming your unique journey into a leadership approach that not only commands respect but also evokes change. It's about inspiring others to follow you not because of your title but because they trust you to lead them down the right path. And remember, respect grows when it is a two-way street; leaders who respect their team will likely have that respect returned in spades.

So, as you take these insights to heart, let them not only guide you toward leadership in general but toward your ultimate goal: becoming a CEO. This journey is yours for the taking if you want it. This book is about allowing you to have choices. Lead with purpose, and let every step forward bring you closer to transforming your professional dreams into reality.

The first step involves ambition. Let's harness yours. Start thinking strategically about which new learning opportunities and promotions will add value to you along the path to the CEO chair.

ABC CALLOUTS

Why is it worth pursuing a CEO position? Let's recap the ABC's of how to plan for the CEO position:

A. **A CEO transforms visions into reality, sparks innovation, and builds a culture that rocks:** If you want to influence business strategies and organizational cultures, provide services or products that serve the needs of people, and even influence social issues, consider becoming a CEO.

B. **Being a successful CEO means having the right mindset:** Embrace visionary thinking, take bold moves, maintain focus during chaos, see opportunities instead of obstacles, develop innovative solutions, and have a relentless drive for excellence.

C. **Communication, decision-making, and emotional intelligence are essential:** Embrace your own growth and cultivate these skills by pursuing continuous learning, seeking out diverse experiences, and drawing inspiration from real-life leaders.

CEO
INSIGHT

*"In the future, there will be no female leaders.
There will just be leaders."*

———

—Sheryl Sandberg, Founder of LeanIn.Org

Chapter 3

THE TRUTH UNVEILED
NAVIGATE THE MAZE TO CEO AND
AVOID THE OBSTACLES ALONG THE WAY

*I*magine this: You're offered a promotion, and, of course, your first instinct is to jump for joy. But wait! Is this really the right path to becoming a CEO? Maybe taking this promotion isn't such a good idea!

In this chapter, we'll dive into the cold, hard facts about promotions and how they can shape your journey to the top. We'll also talk about other facts you need to be aware of.

Now, don't get me wrong. Promotions can be fantastic opportunities for growth and learning. In my own career, I was fortunate to climb the ladder multiple times, each rung offering new challenges and chances to contribute. I was always grateful for those opportunities, but here's the kicker: If I had been laser-focused on the CEO track from the get-go, I might have approached these opportunities differently.

So let's talk about the career strategy for becoming a CEO. What are the secret plays that lead to a win?

Picture this game plan.

For a good warm up, begin with some training in the support or staff side of the business, such as marketing, HR, or public/government relations, to get acquainted with the company's fundamental operations.

Then for extra strength training, move on to a couple of additional stints on the staff side of the business, maybe in business development, strategic planning, finance, technical support, or supply chain management, so you can better support the players on the line.

With this warm up and practice behind you, you're ready for the real game. Now, to ultimately win, you need to play on the line and commercial sides of the business, in operations, product development, and/or sales. Here you'll acquire the skills that will take you to the finish line.

The heavy lifting starts when you become responsible for P&L. That's where the game truly begins. In its most simplistic definition, P&L is the aggregation of revenues, costs, and expenses, which determines if a business is making or losing money. Once you have P&L under your purview, you'll learn what being a CEO is all about and what you'll need in your playbook of experiences to be considered for a CEO role. Unfortunately, not all organizations have multiple positions with P&L responsibility, as many times only the CEO handles P&L. So, if you're lucky enough to get this experience, you'll have an advantage.

Sounds like a winning playbook for the CEO spot, right? It is, but the training can be hard to get, especially for ambitious women like you.

THE STAFF ROLE TRAP

Here's a cold, hard fact that might make you pause: Historically, young women are funneled into staff or support positions early in their careers. These roles—think accounting, IT, HR, public relations (PR), or marketing—are vital support functions that keep the company's engine running smoothly, and beginning your career here is not necessarily a problem. But here's the catch: Staff roles aren't directly involved with the product, service, or customer interactions, a.k.a. line and commercial roles. You might be asking, "What's the problem with that?" Well, staff roles aren't the training grounds for potential CEOs; the training grounds are in the line and commercial roles.

I'd like to explain my understanding of how men *and* women climb the ladder of success. Remember, this is what I've observed. Others may have seen something different, but since you're reading my book, you get my explanation!

Admittedly, not everyone who became a CEO (most of whom are men) had that goal on their radar early on in their careers. However, men in senior-level executive positions often notice other talented young men early in their careers and help those young men chart a career path similar to the one they took.

Unfortunately, in my experience, those same senior executives don't notice as many talented young women. It's not that these young women's talents aren't acknowledged, but often there's a subconscious bias to direct talented women to staff and support roles. This is compounded by the fact that young women see this as the path successful senior executive women in the organization took, some of whom may be C-suite members.

If anyone had seen me as a role model for how to get to the C-suite, they would have seen multiple promotions in increasingly responsible staff and support roles. When I finally joined the C-suite, I was the chief administrative officer.

When you observe successful women early in your career, it looks like an amazing path to follow. After all, no one can argue that these women haven't achieved a certain level of success. I found similar success on this path, and I was proud of myself for having gotten there.

So you might be asking, "What's the problem with this? Won't the path that I take to become part of the C-suite eventually lead to the CEO position?" Statistically, probably not. Why? My path was entirely in support and staff functions, not line and commercial functions, which are essential experiences for a successful CEO.

Now, don't panic if you're in a staff role. Many successful CEOs have worn both hats—line and commercial roles along with some staff positions. The key is finding balance while prioritizing the line/commercial side of the scale. Spending too much time in staff roles early on can make it challenging to switch tracks later. You might need to take a step backward to gain that essential operations or commercial experience.

What do I mean by taking a step backward? For example, say you're a senior manager in a staff function, and you've achieved a certain level of responsibility in that position. To move into a line role from that staff position, you may need to step down to a less senior level, such as being a supervisor in operations reporting to a senior manager (the level you're at today). This may feel like a step backward, and you may get a pay cut in the process. However, if the company wants to "groom" you for a certain role that requires both staff and line experience, they'll find a way to ensure you're treated fairly.

So what's an aspiring CEO to do?

Seek operations and commercial experience early. This is your golden ticket. It may not be your first assignment, but it needs to be in the early stages of your career.

If you're offered a staff position in an exciting industry, go for it—but with a caveat.

Be clear about your ambitions. Tell your supervisor and other management leaders that you're aiming for a line or commercial position in the near future and that your ultimate goal is to land a role with P&L responsibilities. Some companies are organized with multiple P&L centers, while others only give P&L responsibility to one person, i.e., the CEO. Landing a position with successful P&L experience attached to it is a huge jump ahead for you when being considered for a CEO role.

On an episode of *Preparing for the Possibility*, I spoke with Maryann Bruce, an independent director and former Division President and CEO of a Fortune 100 company. We talked about women having P&L responsibility in their roles. Maryann stated:

> "P&L responsibility helps you really dig deep and understand all of the components of what goes into making a product or a service of a company successful. And so that's the number one thing that I believe women need

to do if they aspire to be in the C-suite, particularly the CEO. And unfortunately, many young women don't realize how important that is." [6]

But now you *do* know how important this is. It's certainly intimidating to know the buck stops with you, but, hey, you can do this!

Leverage your mentor (more on this in Chapter 6) and brainstorm strategies to make the transition from a staff role to a line role a reality. Listen to what your mentors say about managing P&L; like many things in life, the more you do it, the more you'll be able to say, "I got this!"

And remember, a brief stint in a support function, particularly one without P&L responsibility, isn't a career killer. But if you're dreaming of that corner office, you'll need to branch out into line and commercial roles sooner rather than later.

Here's your mission, should you choose to accept it: Understand which are the operating, product development, and sales positions in your company and then take a good, hard look at your career path. Are you positioned for a line or commercial role, or are you stuck in the comfort zone of a staff role? It's time to plant those seeds of ambition and cultivate the diverse experiences that will help you bloom into the leader you want to be.

MORE COLD, HARD FACTS

Alright, ladies, it's time to pull back the curtain and face the other truths I've witnessed over three decades in the corporate jungle. Buckle up, because we're about to dive into more of the nitty-gritty of what really goes down in the workplace.

Now, I'm not here to play the blame game or dissect the "whys" of it all. My mission is to give you an insider's peek at the backstage action that shapes careers. Let's get one thing crystal clear: I'm not about pulling men down. Nope. I'm all about lifting women up to stand shoulder-to-shoulder with their male counterparts. I truly believe that we'll all be in a better place when women and men have the same opportunities to succeed. As Melinda French Gates states in her book *The Moment of Lift*, "When you lift up women, you lift up humanity." [7]

By reading this book, I want to share my observations and insights from my years in business concerning women and men. So come in close, because I've got a story that'll knock your power suits off.

Picture this: I'm sitting in my office, having one-on-one career chats with young, bright-eyed employees just like you. In the early years of their careers, both men and women would come in with the same burning question: "What do I need to do to get that next promotion?" Fair enough, right?

But here's where it gets interesting. Fast forward about five years, when these same folks are hitting their early thirties. The women? Still ambitious and asking about that next promotion. But the men? They've changed their tune. Now they're asking, "What do I need to do to become the head of this division?" The head of a division? Wait! You've just begun your career!

Talk about a plot twist!

It's like the men suddenly got an invitation to the "Big Dreams Club," and the women . . . Well, many were still waiting for their invitation. What happened here?

Now, I'm not in any way saying the women were less ambitious and didn't want to succeed. These women and men were equally committed to becoming successful, but somewhere along the line, the men started seeing themselves in those corner offices, while the women were still focusing on the next rung of the ladder. The men had no more experience than the women to make them more qualified, but they saw themselves as ready to make the leap.

Why? Maybe it's a confidence thing, with many men possibly being overly confident and believing they're up for the task while many women aren't as confident and are probably afraid of failure. Maybe it's because women don't see enough women in those top spots. Maybe no one inspired them to ascend to those high roles. Whatever the reason, it's time to change the script.

Here is a quote from another *Preparing for the Possibility* episode I did with Tracey Brophy Warson, the former CEO of Citi Private Bank, North America, that I believe summarizes this phenomena:

> "The biggest mistake women make is we think we need to be 100 percent qualified for the job . . . What are we afraid of? Go for it. Trust yourself and learn." [8]

Great advice. Let's start with some of the basics so you can gain the confidence to trust yourself.

TAKE A SEAT AT THE TABLE AND PROJECT YOUR VOICE

Alright, ladies, let's talk meetings. I know you've heard this before, but it bears repeating—and I'm going to give it to you straight.

Here's the deal: If you're invited to a meeting, it's not because they need someone to warm the chair. You're invited because someone thinks you've got something valuable to bring to the table. And speaking of tables, take a seat at it, for crying out loud! Don't sit by the wall!

I'm not being metaphorical here. I've seen far too many young women hanging back and deferring to others. Stop it. Right now.

I get that there's a pecking order. The big cheeses usually have their favorite spots. You'll figure out quickly which seats are off-limits. But once you find an empty spot, plant yourself at that table. No back row for you. No wallflower act. You need to be seen and heard just like everyone else in that room.

Act like you're a player in this game because, guess what? You are.

And for the love of all things holy, come prepared. If reading material is sent out beforehand, read it. When the meeting starts, focus. This isn't the time to be planning your next meeting or worrying about your to-do list.

Got a question? Ask it. And when you do, channel your inner actress. Project your voice. I know some of us have naturally softer voices, but in the boardroom, that can be mistaken for a lack of confidence. So speak up, speak clearly, and make yourself heard. Don't forget to make eye contact when you speak, including with the senior people. This isn't the time to be intimidated. Project confidence, and others will pay attention to what you have to say.

In a *Preparing for the Possibility* episode, I spoke with Jocelyn Mangan, the founder of illumyn Impact (formerly Him for Her). She had a great comment about women needing to feel more comfortable asking questions:

> "When you have that feeling in your gut that you really have something to say and it might actually be the different opinion or it might be the different perspective, that's exactly the right time to speak up." [9]

Don't be a victim of groupthink. Be brave and speak up. Senior leaders will take notice when they know you aren't afraid of going against the masses.

Now, let me tell you what happened to me too many times in my career when I wasn't fast enough to speak up. I'd wait for the "perfect moment" to ask my brilliant question. And you know what happened? Someone else beat me to it. They'd ask my question and get praised for being "insightful." Talk about a kick in the teeth. But whose fault was that? Mine.

So here's the bottom line: Ask those thoughtful questions. Get noticed. The more you do it, the easier it gets. Trust me on this one. It took me years to figure this out, and that's why I'm telling you now. Be brave and speak up! You can do this. But as Adrian Bracy, the former CEO of the YWCA of Metro St. Louis, said,

"Don't tell the whole story . . . cut to the punchline!" [10]

Be succinct and get to the point. Don't lose your audience's interest because you've added too many unnecessary details.

In a *Preparing for the Possibility* episode I did with Margo Cook, the former President of Nuveen Advisory Services, she had this to say about young women in meetings:

"There's a tendency when you're younger to think you have to fade into the background and that we don't really want to hear your voice. The reality is, especially today with the massive change that's happened in the work environment because of technology, we want to understand what younger people are thinking." [11]

There you go. Those senior leaders want to hear from you!

But what do you do if someone challenges you in a meeting? Let's talk about one of the most important skills for both meetings and leadership: debating.

In the business world, especially at the top, it's all about making decisions. Some are easy, while others are like trying to untangle a ball of yarn while wearing boxing gloves.

Here's the thing: What's clear as day to you might be foggy to someone else. That's where your debating skills come in.

To be a killer debater, here's what you need to do:

- Know your stuff inside and out. No winging-it allowed.
- Look at the problem from all angles. Be the Sherlock Holmes of problem-solving.
- Have an argument so convincing it could sell ice to someone living in the Arctic.

But remember, we're talking about a debate here, not an episode of *Jerry Springer*. Keep your cool. A great debater stays calm and collected despite differing opinions. That's how you earn respect. I've seen too many women duck out of these verbal sparring matches, and let me tell you, that's a one-way ticket to Nowheresville if you're gunning for that CEO spot. You've got to get comfortable jumping into the fray. Analyze that situation like Agathe Christie on steroids. Take a stand like you're planting your flag on the moon. Back it up with cold, hard facts that would make a statistician weep with joy. Never let a debate get personal, and never take it personally when it is directed at you.

Don't just talk—listen. Really listen. Weigh every bit of info like it's solid gold because sometimes, just sometimes, someone else might have a point. (I know, shocking, right?) You have to know when you're in the wrong, and when that happens (hopefully rarely), be a good sport. It's not the end of the world.

Here's your game plan: Choose your position in a debate and defend it like it's the game point. But when your opponent throws you a curveball (and trust me, they will), don't just stand there with your jaw on the floor. Present your position with confidence, and then at the end, regardless of the direction the team decides to go, get on the bandwagon and move on. Being a team player is a skill, too. Don't lose sight of that.

SAYING "YES" TO CHALLENGES

Listen up, ladies! Let's talk about challenges. All the top-notch CEOs I've known didn't just accept challenges—they practically salivated over them. If you want that corner office, you've got to learn to love pushing boundaries. And guess what? That means embracing challenges like they're your new best friends.

I could always spot the future superstars on my team. They were the ones who would hear about a gnarly problem with a crazy deadline and their eyes would light up like a kid in a candy shop. These were the "can-do" rock stars that everyone was fighting to have on their team.

Let me tell you another little secret I've learned over the years: The ones who make it to the top never, ever start by saying, "No, we can't do that." Instead, they say, "Let me see how we might make that happen." Those are the magic words that open doors to bigger and better things.

I'm not saying you should promise the moon and stars if you can't deliver, but don't shoot down ideas before you've even considered them. Do your homework and see what's possible.

SEE A PROBLEM, HAVE A SOLUTION

As you grow into the roles you take on, you'll inevitably face challenges. These moments are golden opportunities to sharpen your problem-solving skills.

If you want to stand out as a leader, master the art of problem-solution presentations. Don't just dump problems on your manager's desk. Instead, present them with thoughtful solutions. "Always present problems with potential solutions" should be one of your eternal mantras.

Spotting problems is child's play, but the real test is dissecting the cause and crafting solutions. And I'm not talking about half-baked ideas. Bring multiple well-researched options to the table. Break down the pros and cons of each approach and highlight your recommended course of action.

This level of analysis shows you're not just another cog in the machine. (Of course you aren't!) You're a forward-thinker, someone who's already operating at a higher level. It screams "future leader" louder than any power suit ever could.

In an interview on *Preparing for the Possibility*, Stacy Since, the founder and former CEO of RISE Collaborative Workspace and a TEDx Speaker, had this to say about problem solving:

> "It's taking that step and giving something a try that makes a difference, and I think the skills of problem solving is what set me up for success as a CEO." [12]

Remember, if you're gunning for more responsibility, flexing both your problem-spotting and solution-crafting muscles sets you apart and gets you noticed.

So the next time you encounter a hurdle, don't just point it out. Roll up your sleeves, dig into the details, and come prepared with solutions. That's how you become indispensable, and that's your ticket to the top.

Here's your next assignment: Become the go-to person who's always crafting solutions, not just identifying problems. Trust me, your coworkers and bosses will notice. They'll start seeing you as the one who's always got an idea up her sleeve, always ready to tackle the next big challenge.

CEOs are problem solvers; it's time for you to become a problem solver, too.

CONFIDENCE: WE ALL WANT IT, BUT HOW DO WE GET IT?

How many times have you heard this? Why are some of us naturally confident, while some, let's just say, have to work on it?

In an episode of the *Women in Finance* podcast I did with Noreen Doyle—the first woman to chair the British Bankers Association and former board chair for Credit Suisse International and Newmont Mining Corporation—she had this to say about confidence:

> "Maybe it's not surprising, but if I had one thing to do over, I would have had an infusion of self-confidence in my early thirties. I discovered later in life that you can actually develop confidence by practice, and it's a bit like acting. If you project confidence, even if you don't feel it, it begins to be a comfortable state, and that projection of confidence is very important to moving into senior roles. If I had one piece of advice: Pretend you're confident, you will become confident." [13]

How's that from a woman who was a super-achiever!

So, if you don't believe you're naturally confident, you aren't alone. But this doesn't mean you aren't confident. You just have to practice, and not too long after, it will be who you are without any acting.

BUSINESS ATTIRE . . . IS THERE SUCH A THING?

Time for another cold, hard fact. I get asked all the time, "Should I be concerned with the clothes I wear to work?" My solution to this is simple. Look up at the successful senior leaders in your organization, and there's your answer. As much as I would like to tell you, "Be yourself! Don't worry what other people think!" that would probably be leading you in the wrong direction.

If you want to tip the scales in your favor when it comes to upward advancement, look around you. Wearing a designer suit when everyone else is in jeans and a T-shirt or wearing jeans and a T-shirt when everyone else is dressed up may not be the best plan. You might be asking, "Is clothing a deal-breaker?" If you're so good at what you do that what you wear won't be noticed, go for it.

But do you really want to take that chance?

Right or wrong, people's opinions matter, and you can't change that. After you become CEO, you'll have more freedom to dress however you want, or you could change the dress code entirely. Until then, I suggest you look around to decide what is right for you now.

THE BALANCING ACT: FAMILY COMMITMENTS, LIFE, AND YOUR CAREER

Many women who became CEOs did it while raising children. You might be wondering, "How can I become a CEO while raising children and still have work-life balance?" As Daisy Dowling, an executive coach, once said, "If it takes a village to raise a child, your job is to build and manage that village the same way you would a project team at work. Get enough people on the team, and make sure their skills are complementary." [14]

In my discussions with women who were mothers and CEOs, there was one common denominator: They all had a strong support system of childcare providers. Maybe it was a partner or spouse, a family member, a friend, or a childcare professional, but they all knew that they weren't alone in caring for their children.

There isn't any one "right" answer to this, but the bottom line is that taking on a leadership position and becoming a mother both come with added responsibilities. There are numerous articles and books written on this subject, and I suggest you learn from the insights of others who have been there and done that.

But there is good news! Being a mother and being a CEO aren't mutually exclusive. Others who came before you have made it possible, and you can, too. You're a smart woman. You'll figure this out.

These are all truths you need to consider as you advance your career. Some are easier to deal with than others, but you don't have to do it all at once. Each truth represents another step for you on your journey to becoming a CEO.

ABC CALLOUTS

Navigating the path to CEO is like setting a course through uncharted waters. There's no single map to follow, but there are always stars to steer by. Don't get caught in the traps of settling for just any promotion. Make your promotions count toward the credentials of becoming a CEO. Let's recap the essential beacons that will guide your journey:

A. **All roles are not created equal:** Seek line and commercial roles in operations, product development, sales experience, and roles with P&L responsibilities—they're your compass to CEO. Don't get stuck in back-office roles, where many women find themselves. It rarely leads to the corner office.

B. **Be a person who takes a seat at the table:** Project your voice, make great eye-contact, engage in the moment, ask relevant questions, and practice debating issues. These skills will help you navigate complex situations.

C. **Challenges are opportunities:** Say "yes" to challenges, and use your creative juices. You may not immediately have a solution, but staying optimistic is extremely important in becoming a leader. Remember, when presenting a problem, always have a solution ready. These traits let others see you as the "go-to" person everyone wants on their team.

CEO
INSIGHT

*"The only impossible journey
is the one you never begin."*

———

—Tony Robbins, author and motivational speaker

Chapter 4

SOW THE SEEDS
OF THE FUTURE

BEGIN WITH INTENT AND
WATCH YOUR LEADERSHIP GROW

You might be asking, "Why should I be thinking now about someday securing a position that isn't in my immediate future? Even if I could become a CEO, isn't it a little early for me to be considering this when I'm only in the first few years of my career?"

I interviewed Irl Engelhardt, the former CEO of Peabody Energy (and one of the two CEOs I reported to), and he had this to say about planning a career:

> "No matter where you start, set lofty goals. Learn what you
> are good at and what you enjoy. As you continue in your

career and gain experience, adjust your goals to reflect your life circumstances. And always remain flexible." [15]

Setting your sights on becoming a CEO is a lofty goal, so I say . . . start your journey there!

We've established the influence that the CEO position carries and why it's worth aspiring toward. Now it's time for you to start planting these CEO seeds.

To get from where you are now to where you want to be—sitting confidently in that CEO chair—you have to dream of a future filled with continuous learning, a healthy dose of planning, and a whole lot of risk-taking. This isn't a path you leave to chance.

Setting your sights on becoming a CEO isn't just about leading a company but about leading a movement. (Think influencer, but on an even bigger scale.) As a CEO, you have the unique opportunity to drive change, sway industries, and make a meaningful impact on the world. It's about having a vision that extends beyond the boardroom and inspires others to join in a shared purpose.

If you've ever been part of a college club, sports team, or a community organization, do you remember how rewarding it was to take part in bringing about change? Multiply that feeling several times over and you'll know what it feels like to be a CEO.

I once asked a friend of mine who is a former CEO what qualities he believed helped him remain relevant during his decades-long tenure. His answer was simple: "Always be adaptable to change, and never stop learning." Mona Andrews, the founder and CEO of Stay in the Game, agreed in the *Preparing for the Possibility* episode we did together:

"We need to be very comfortable being uncomfortable . . . always pushing to grow." [16]

Remember this—we'll talk more about these concepts later.

CRAFTING YOUR LEADERSHIP VISION AND VALUES

Female CEOs are still relatively rare, particularly in publicly traded companies. Despite progress in recent years, women remain under-represented in top leadership positions within most industries. In 2025, less than 10 percent of the CEOs of leading Fortune 500 companies are women.

With those odds, do you ever wonder how some of the most inspiring female CEOs got to where they are? It all starts with a clear leadership vision.

Not just any vision but one that fires you up and is drenched in your passion and purpose.

Setting ambitious career goals isn't about scribbling down "become a CEO" on a sticky note. Any CEO reading this is likely laughing at this idea. It's about dreaming big while grounding that dream in what really lights you up inside. You need to feel passionate about your dream.

What's that one thing you could talk about for hours, the thing that makes you leap out of bed in the morning? Think about this. That's where your vision starts.

But here's the kicker—your vision needs to vibe with your *values*. A truly successful CEO can accomplish great things because what they do feels right to them. It comes naturally; they aren't following someone else's agenda. They follow their own values, confident in themselves and what they want to accomplish.

It's like building a puzzle. Every piece needs to fit to see the whole picture. Your career isn't just a series of jobs and accomplishments; it's a reflection of who you are, what you stand for, and the stamp you hope to make on the world.

Remember what I said about creating yourself, just like the quote from George Bernard Shaw? That's the dream you need to recognize early in your career.

This is where that idea becomes reality. Crafting a leadership vision means weaving your personal values tightly into your professional aspirations. It's about making choices that resonate with your core, choices that feel right deep down in your gut.

Over the years, I've watched many talented individuals "fail" at a company, only to move on and succeed at another. "How can that be?" you might ask. Just as we're all different as individuals, companies are also different from one another. Every organization's culture is unique. There's no "right" or "wrong" culture. Some of us might feel more comfortable in Culture A, while others prefer Culture B. Understanding your vision and values is crucial to finding where you can succeed.

But practically, how do you start creating a leadership vision?

A great first step is to look at the leaders who inspire you, who are living their best lives, and reflect on their style and accomplishments. What makes them special to you? Is it their values, what they have accomplished, or how they interact with others?

Your task is to see what you admire in other leaders and to start sketching out your own leadership vision. Your vision shouldn't simply imitate someone else. Instead, it should answer these questions:

- What impact do I want to have?
- How do I want to influence the world around me?
- And, very importantly, what legacy do I want to leave?

Remember, this vision is your North Star, guiding you through choices, challenges, and changes.

Next, define your values. Ask yourself:
- What principles do I hold most dear?
- In tough situations, what guides my decision-making?
- How do I define success beyond titles and accomplishments?

By aligning your passion, purpose, and values with your vision, you're not only preparing to become a CEO, you're gearing up to be a leader who leaves a legacy.

An exercise I found useful (albeit a little too late in my career) was to prepare a summary of what I'd like others to write or say about me and what I accomplished. Let's call it a Career Eulogy. Write something about yourself that you would like others to be able to say about you in a Career Eulogy. Take the time to do this and focus on the type of leader you want others to see in you and what you plan to accomplish.

Craft a vision that's so *you* that it can't help but propel you toward that CEO role, transforming you from a dreamer into a doer and, ultimately, into a leader who inspires the current and next generation. As Beth Chesterton, the founder of The Ignite Method and my managing partner at ABC to CEO, often reminds young women,

> "Potential begins the minute you stop focusing on your fear that you are not enough and start focusing on bringing all you've got to the job at hand." [17]

WHAT DOES LEADERSHIP PRESENCE LOOK LIKE ON YOU?

Ever wonder if you've got the leadership aura? Here's a litmus test: Are people following you because they want to or because their paycheck depends on it?

On an episode of *Preparing for the Possibility*, I interviewed Kathy Mazzarella, the CEO of Graybar. One of the insightful things she said about leadership that stuck with me was this:

"As a leader, it's not about you . . . *ever*!" [18]

She understood the assignment—leadership is about where you're taking your team.

True leaders have a magnetic pull. People follow them because they trust where their leader is taking them. These leaders don't need to abuse their authority to get things done. Instead, they paint a vision so vivid and compelling that folks can't help but jump on board. It's like they're handing out tickets to the most exciting trip in town. Everyone wants in.

When the journey gets tough, these leaders don't break a sweat. They stay calm and keep a steady hand on the wheel. True leaders make their team feel like they could weather any storm, but they're not trying to be superheroes. They know their kryptonite and surround themselves with people who can fill in the gaps.

If you're not oozing charisma from every pore, don't worry. You can cultivate leadership mojo. But forget about cookie-cutter approaches. You've got to find your own groove, your authentic leadership style.

Remember, the real test comes when you glance over your shoulder. If you see a parade of fired-up folks who follow you not because HR told them to but because they believe in you and your vision, then congratulations! You're doing something right.

True leadership isn't about barking orders from on high. It's about communicating a direction and inspiring people to reach for the stars alongside you.

So are you ready to become the kind of leader people choose to follow?

GETTING OUT OF THE OFFICE

One of the mistakes I see people make is getting too comfortable staying "in their own world," be that a home office, a cubicle/work office, or an assigned work area. If you don't work from home, make a conscious effort to interact with your coworkers. (You've got this!) Although phone conversations and video calls are convenient when a sudden issue pops up, there's nothing like a personal interaction to go beyond the immediate situation and get to the root of the problem.

And if you work in an organization with multiple locations, visiting and meeting people from those locations will give you opportunities that you never would have gotten if you stayed in your own office. So get out of your comfort zone! The more people who get to know you beyond a voice on a phone or a face on a video screen, the greater your influence can be.

TAKE CALCULATED RISKS

Jenny Just is one of the most successful women in business. She's also one of the few self-made female billionaires in the world. In 1997, she cofounded a fintech empire, PEAK6, with her partner, starting with $1.5M in seed money and growing it into a multibillion-dollar financial services and technology giant. Taking risks is one of the ways she built her companies. With her daughter, Juliette, she has also cofounded a nonprofit organization called Poker Power, which teaches women about the obstacles and strategies to being successful in business. I highly recommend you look into it.

One of the issues Poker Power deals with centers around the idea that women need to get comfortable with taking risks. In a *Preparing for the Possibility* episode I did with Jenny, she said:

> "If you never play your cards, you will lose. The opposite is also true . . . If you only play your best cards, you will also lose." [19]

Jenny is a firm proponent that opportunity only comes from taking risks, something she believes many people, especially women, are somewhat uncomfortable doing, but with practice it can become a little easier.

Good leaders take calculated risks, which means having a risk-taking mindset. The two go hand-in-hand. Risk-taking is essential for leadership growth, and leadership is more successful when you take calculated risks. That mindset, once developed, can be a seed that will continue to grow and flourish throughout your career.

Taking risks helps you develop resilience and adaptability, two crucial qualities for any leader. By taking risks early on, you can learn to navigate uncertainty and bounce back from setbacks, preparing yourself for the challenges you'll continue to face as you climb the leadership ladder.

Taking risks opens doors to new opportunities and experiences that you may not have gotten otherwise. We've all been in situations that gave us anxiety at first, but when we look back, we see a silver lining that we may have missed. And sometimes it takes the unpleasant experience of weathering a storm to find that silver lining.

The ability to embrace calculated risks is one of the most important traits for any aspiring leader—especially a future CEO.

Now, I'm not talking about the foolish, jump-off-a-cliff-without-a-parachute kind of risk. No, I mean the calculated leaps that push you beyond your comfort zone.

I did a podcast episode with Lauren Herring, the CEO of IMPACT Group, and here's what she had to say about learning behaviors that may not come naturally:

> "The more you do something that is uncomfortable, the more comfortable you get with it." [20]

We've all experienced this in our lives outside of business. Remember how scary it was when you first learned how to drive a car or when you first spoke in front of a group of people? For me, these activities were very uncomfortable, but the more I did them, the more comfortable I became.

The same is true in business. Whenever I was given a new responsibility that I knew little about, I wondered how I would ever master it. But I always did, and then I knew it was time to move on. Being uncomfortable doesn't mean there's a problem, it just means you have a learning curve to conquer.

Growth and comfort cannot coexist because growth inherently requires you to step outside of your comfort zone. To grow as a leader, you must embrace new challenges and confront the unfamiliar. Staying within the boundaries of comfort limits your opportunities for development and keeps you stagnant. Discomfort is a sign of growth. Don't think discomfort means you're doing something wrong.

In an interview I did with Jeane Hull, a former C-suite executive and currently an independent director for several boards, she told me:

> "You'll always feel levels of discomfort when you are taking on new challenges. You'll feel a bit intimidated, but that's normal." [21]

The discomfort that accompanies growth and transformation is more common than you realize. Don't think that you are alone in this and or that it means you aren't CEO material. Countless people have felt the same way, including those who became CEOs.

Another *Preparing for the Possibility episode* I did was with Jenny Johnson, the president and CEO of Franklin Templeton Investments. Her comment on risks is very relevant and, in my opinion, particularly for women. Jenny stated:

> "If you find yourself thinking that you want to do something, and you find yourself being the one talking yourself out of why you're capable of doing it, *stop* and say, 'Go for it, I'm going to take that risk.'" [22]

So what's your risk?

Maybe it's pitching a new idea to your team, speaking up and debating when you disagree with something, applying for a job that feels out of reach, or leading a project that pushes you into uncharted territory. Whatever it is, stepping out of your comfort zone leads to growth.

Start looking for opportunities to take calculated risks today. It's in these moments of discomfort and uncertainty that real growth happens.

Let me share another secret to success: Every challenge you face head-on opens doors to opportunities you never imagined. These moments of risk are about more than success or failure; they're about discovering your resilience and your adaptability. The more doors you open, the greater your leadership potential becomes. Every challenge you face and overcome will give you the confidence to deal with your next challenge.

And even if you take a risk and don't fully succeed, pushing yourself after a perceived failure strengthens your ability to keep going when it gets tough the next time. You won't always succeed, but your stamina to continue despite the setback is growth in and of itself.

Embracing risk isn't just a part of the leadership journey; it's the essence of becoming a CEO. It's about making decisions when the path isn't clear, evaluating the options, standing firm in the face of uncertainty after making a decision and learning to trust your judgment.

Remember, the leaders who make history are the ones who aren't afraid to rewrite the rules and venture into the unknown. Leaders who make history are the ones who believe in the possibility of what could be.

IT'S ALL ABOUT STRATEGIC THINKING

As an aspiring CEO, another important skill you need to cultivate is strategic thinking. Early on in your career, you'll have limited opportunity to participate in strategic thinking and planning discussions. However, becoming aware of your company's short-term and long-term strategic plans will show you what strategic thinking is all about. These plans take the strategic thinking of the executives and board of directors and set the direction for the future—they chart a course through complex and ever-changing landscapes. It is how an organization plans to secure their success in the future.

But what exactly is strategic thinking, and how do you develop it? At its core, strategic thinking is the ability to look into the future and see the big picture—to look beyond the day-to-day operations and tactical challenges and to focus on the long-term vision and what goals your organization needs to implement to achieve that vision. It's about being able to anticipate future trends, identify emerging opportunities and threats, and make proactive decisions that will position your company for success.

It's about your company living its best life. And it happens through great strategic thinking and outcomes.

In sports, strategic thinking it's about predicting where the ball is going to go before it goes there. Strategic planning is about what you're going to do now knowing where the ball is going!

In developing a strategic plan, your company's senior executives have to understand the key drivers of success in the industry and determine what are the biggest challenges and opportunities facing the industry. Understanding your company's unique strengths and capabilities and developing a plan to leverage those strengths to create a sustainable competitive advantage is critical.

One important aspect of strategic thinking is staying on top of what your competitors are doing. You need to keep your finger on your business's pulse to see how healthy it is and how you can improve it. Get in the habit of reading publications and news articles about your industry.

Strategic planning is not only about what you and others in your organization believe the future may hold, it's also about what your competitors are seeing and doing in the meantime. Acquisitions and divestitures are born from evaluating opportunities to improve an organization's business performance. Even early on in your career, it's important to begin to understand the industry-wide picture and with it, where the competitive advantage lies.

One powerful tool for beginning to hone your own strategic thinking skills is scenario planning with your team. This involves systematically exploring your team's functional purpose and its possible futures. You need to know why your team exists. By considering a wide range of potential outcomes, from best-case to worst-case scenarios, you can identify the key factors that will shape your team's future.

Ask yourself, "What would happen if my department no longer existed? What can we do to add value beyond our current contributions?" Look outside of your organization to see how other successful companies handle your department's functions. Ask other departments in your organization what they think about your department's contributions. Research if there's a more cost-effective way for your department to provide the same service, such as by implementing AI or simplifying your processes. Considering and responding to questions of this nature will allow you to begin honing your strategic thinking skills.

Now let's take it a step forward. Another key aspect of strategic thinking is the ability to think systemically—to understand how your team and other teams are both interconnected and interdependent. This means looking beyond your own functional area or business unit and considering how decisions and actions in one part of the company ripple throughout the entire system.

You may want to consider talking to colleagues in other departments to better understand what their department does and how they impact the core business. Here are some talking points to kick off the conversation:

- Do you understand the supply chain side of your business? What problems are they encountering, and how do they plan to react to them?
- What about the business development team? What can you learn from them regarding the company's future growth opportunities?
- The financial planning team is always considering projected financial results. I think it's interesting to see how their forecasts provide support for future decisions and directions made by the company.
- What about government relations? What may be happening from a societal perspective that might impact your organization?
- What about operations? What efficiencies in technology could be implemented that are not being used today?
- And sales? What will our customers need in the future that will change the product/services we produce today?

And the list goes on.

These are just a few examples of the types of issues across the organization that you'll need to understand when formulating a strategic plan for the future.

Developing your strategic thinking skills also requires challenging assumptions and conventional wisdom. Just because something has always been done a certain way doesn't mean it's the best way—or the only way. By cultivating a curious and open-minded approach and actively seeking out new perspectives and ideas, you can break free from old patterns and find innovative solutions to complex challenges.

Of course, mastering strategic thinking is an ongoing process—one that requires continuous observations and evaluations. But by investing in your own development, you'll be well-equipped to be an integral member of your team today and become the leader of your team tomorrow.

Strategic thinking is a powerful skill that often takes years of experience to develop. As you climb the ladder in your organization, the strategic thinking skills that you're honing now will evolve and pave the way for an even broader range of strategic thinking in the future.

CHANNEL YOUR LEADERSHIP STYLE

Establishing clear leadership vision and values, keeping a vibrant circle of change-agents around you, always learning, and becoming comfortable taking calculated risks—these are all necessary steps in your journey toward the pinnacle of leadership: the CEO role.

The path to CEO is paved with many unknowns, but your relentless drive to make an impact will get you there.

The journey to CEO starts with a decision—a decision to embrace your potential, lead with intention, and carve a path that others will aspire to follow. The world is waiting for CEOs like you. Sow the seeds of your future now at the beginning of your journey.

ABC CALLOUTS

Here's a quick recap of the ABC's to planting the seed on your path to becoming a CEO:

A. **Articulate the leader you want to become:** Consider your personal values and what energizes you. Study the leaders you admire. You are responsible for becoming the type of leader you can be proud of.

B. **Be prepared to take risks:** Fearing risks will stifle your upward progress. Challenge yourself to step beyond the familiar, understanding that true leadership is often found in moments of uncertainty. Remain adaptable when your path changes.

C. **Cultivate strategic thinking:** Evaluate what your team needs now and how it needs to adapt to the future. Learn how other departments within your company think strategically. Don't settle for the status quo. If you don't see a path to making something better, someone else will.

CEO
INSIGHT

"If your actions inspire others to dream more, learn more, do more, and become more, you are a leader."

_____

—John Quincy Adams, sixth President of the United States

Chapter 5

LEAVE A LEGACY
CRAFT YOUR UNIQUE CONTRIBUTION
TO THE WORLD

What makes you shine as a leader? How do you differentiate yourself from others?

Shining as a leader is about much more than snagging a fancy title or climbing the corporate ladder. It's about the vibe you bring, how you bounce back from setbacks, the paths you pave, and how others can depend on you to always go above and beyond to get the job done.

Your leadership journey is your personal masterpiece, showcasing your unique flair in every position you hold and every decision you make. It's about leaving a legacy that stands out, positively impacts those around you, and paves the way for the future.

So what's your signature leadership style going to be? Why will people follow and remember you?

Maybe it's your knack for seeing the silver lining in tough times, your way of rallying folks who trust where you're going, or your never-say-die attitude that keeps you going during a crisis. Maybe it's the way you handle conflict, your integrity, or how you break down a complicated situation into straightforward terms. Your journey to becoming a CEO is as distinctive as you are, and it's your one-of-a-kind leadership style that'll not only shape your career but etch your legacy. So let's get started creating that legacy!

In a *Preparing for the Possibility* episode I did with Bisa Grant, the CEO of Anchor, a municipal construction and project management company, she stated:

> "To be a leader is not just telling somebody what to do or necessarily showing somebody how to do it, it's also inspiring them to do the right thing, to do good work. And you have to find within yourself what inspires you to be the best version of you so that you can be that example for others that are coming up behind you." [23]

So let's mold a leadership vibe so uniquely you that it inspires *everyone*. Your impact can ripple far beyond your immediate circle, so step into your leadership light and let it steer your course. It's your time to leave a mark, not only as a leader but as a beacon of innovation, insight, and resilience. The journey to CEO is about the impact you have and the transformations you spark along the way.

MASTERING THE BASICS . . . AT EVERY LEVEL

Before you can leave a mark, you need to master the basics. Effective leadership isn't just born, it's built from the ground up, starting with the fundamental skills that many overlook in their rush to the top. Some of us come by these skills naturally, and some of us have to develop them.

Think of it this way: Very few successful industry pioneers or CEOs who have reshaped the landscape started with a grand vision executed flawlessly on their first try.

Instead, they built their legacy and following on a foundation of solid skills they learned and honed over time through proactive learning. They tapped into various platforms for new knowledge, studied the world around them to understand different perspectives, and pursued creative endeavors to sharpen their innovative thinking. And in every role they assumed, they left behind a trail of great performances.

Let's begin with some advice to help you where you are right now on your path to CEO and to give you some insight into where your adventure may take you.

And keep in mind that this adventure won't be easy. Getting there involves work, solid results, and commitment.

JUST STARTING OUT . . . YOUR ADVENTURE IS ABOUT TO BEGIN

You're at the beginning of your career, and you've been working in your industry for five to ten years. You've taken on a number of assignments and nailed each one with a stellar performance. At this stage, you're still absorbing a lot of information and learning the ropes of your industry. For instance, you might be learning about your industry's latest technologies, your organization's unique methodologies, or essential regulations in your field. Or you might still be exploring different career paths within or outside your industry. If you're in marketing, you could try out roles in digital marketing, content creation, or market research to find your niche, for example. Or if you're in health care, you might consider pivoting to hospitality, PR, or financial services. This is when you start honing in on what you enjoy and what fits your values.

In an episode of *Preparing for the Possibility* I did with Andra Kidd, the CEO of Spheros Environmental, she said:

> "Even if you have one track you want to go on, that doesn't mean that you have to do that for the rest of your career." [24]

Many CEOs had many paths that led to their success.

CORE SKILLS

Focus on building foundational skills such as communication, problem-solving, and adaptability, all of which will help you develop your own leadership style.

A quick note about the term "leadership style." Leadership styles are often segregated into these common categories: democratic, authoritative, bureaucratic, visionary, coaching, and laissez-faire. You can read about each of these (and a few others) in detail on many websites.

Most leaders I've known don't consciously decide to be a certain type of leader. Instead, they evolve into what often comes naturally for them. And some leaders can adapt their style depending on the situation.

When I refer to leadership style in this book, my intent isn't to propose you adopt any particular style but to illustrate the different types of successful leaders and help you determine which direction best fits your values and personality. Even then, your own leadership style will likely evolve over time.

Now let's get back to foundational skills. To be an effective leader, you need to master the basics, no matter where you're headed. Successful CEOs are visionaries who can adapt, decide, innovate, compete, build teams, manage ambiguity, are great negotiators, and take calculated risks. Their personal attributes also often include being accountable, inspirational, confident, driven, empathetic, and optimistic.

Sounds like only a superperson could master such a long list. However, since most of us don't excel in all of these skills, we need to recognize which skills we're comfortable with and which we're lacking. And for the skills we need but either don't possess or don't have the time to acquire, we need to surround ourselves with others who excel in those areas. Odds are you won't master every skill, so recognizing this is important. This is also the time to identify mentors who can help us either acquire those skills or supplement our shortcomings with other experts. More on mentors in Chapter 6.

No CEO is an expert at everything. In an interview I did with Kim Popovitz, the CEO of Genomic Health, she explains this with an analogy of an orchestra conductor.[25] Conductors can't play every instrument in the orchestra, but they can lead a group of musicians who are experts in many different instruments, and together they create great music. Without a competent team, the conductor only has a vision of what can be. For the vision to become reality, the conductor needs people who each possess a special talent to bring their musical vision to life. No conductor can create music without the whole orchestra. Kim also explained that if you try to do things that you should be delegating, your staff may believe you don't trust them—trust is a huge component of building successful relationships between both individuals and teams.

The conductor trusts the players to perform not only what is expected of them but to give their best for the performance. As leaders, we need to remember this, especially when we get tempted to do too many things ourselves. We all need an "orchestra" to attain our goals.

Your role as a CEO will be to craft your vision and determine what kind of team you'll need to make your vision a reality.

ADVICE

As you progress in your career, you'll continue to develop your leadership style and understand what builds upon your natural strengths. There are many ways to learn about effective leadership models. You can participate in programs, read books, and, perhaps most importantly, observe successful leaders. At this stage of your career, you may even be facing the trials and errors of leading a team, whether it's your existing colleagues or a brand new team that's been assigned to you.

Diving into opportunities that expand your analytical thinking sharpens your ability to interpret data and make informed decisions when solving problems. Read studies of business cases, both those that succeeded and those that failed, and develop a strong foundation in market trends and operational efficiencies to expand your business acumen.

A FEW PIECES OF CRITICAL ADVICE

OK, remember how in the beginning of this book, I warned you that certain things bear repeating to make sure you understand them? This is one of them.

If you're aiming for the CEO chair, beware . . . not all promotions are created equal! I hope you learn a lot from this book, but if there's only one thing I want you to remember, this is it: Don't let well-intentioned career moves become obstacles to your success.

Well-run administrative/support/staff roles within an organization are an important component to a thriving company. The CEOs I worked for all understood the value of the financial, HR, legal, supply chain, IT, public, and government relation teams to name a few examples. These teams keep the company's wheels in motion so the operations, product development, and sales teams can operate the most effectively.

A successful CEO understands this balance and stays attuned to what all these teams need to maximize the company's performance.

A rotation in several administrative roles is an ideal way to better understand the ins and outs of how the business functions as a whole. But in the end, keep these assignments short. Too much time spent in administrative roles will be detrimental to your goal of becoming a CEO.

This is precisely where too many young women like you get assigned and, quite honestly, get stuck. Remember, a career of successful performance in staff positions won't necessarily lead to the CEO chair. Although becoming a CEO wasn't on my radar, my successful career in support functions would have kept me from becoming a realistic competitor for the CEO position, compared to others whose careers included core experiences in operations, product development, sales, and the highly coveted P&L roles.

Finally, if you aren't in a line/commercial position after the first ten or so years of your career, you need to let your organization know about your goal. Once you land a line or commercial role, it's all about your performance. To keep moving up the ladder and obtaining the experience you need to be considered for CEO, you must have a track record of success. I cannot stress enough how important this is on your path to becoming a CEO.

You need to proactively position yourself for success!

WHAT'S UP NEXT . . . A PEEK AT YOUR FUTURE

OK, let's take a break and have a little bit of fun here. It's time for some dreaming!

Let's look into a crystal ball to see what you need to be doing in the next decade of your career. This will help you map out a possible path to CEO. Make the wrong turn, and you could end up like I did—in an executive seat at the table (albeit one I *did* enjoy) but not one that would have led to being CEO. Even if I'd never made it to the CEO position, I would have been a better leader overall if I had experience in the operations and commercial side of the business.

Michael Altshuler, a career coach and motivational speaker, wrote, "The bad news is time flies. The good news is you are the pilot." [26] I like this quote because it highlights how you don't have to wait to decide later in your career if you want to pursue becoming a CEO. Take the pilot seat and set your course now. It's time for you to live your best life!

Here's my advice: Start preparing now to give yourself the chance to decide later if that's a course you want to take. When you're in your twenties, it seems like you have a long career ahead of you. However, the plans you make today will impact the career choices you have available tomorrow. Preparing for the CEO role doesn't mean that you have to take it if you decide on a different career path down the road. But deciding later that you do want it without the proper experience will likely keep you from getting it. As a *Wall Street Journal* article reported on September 17, 2024, a ten year study by LeanIn.org and researchers at McKinsey found that people who only had experience in staff roles were less likely to become CEOs.[27]

My goal in writing this book is to ensure you understand the basics of the journey to become a CEO. Ultimately, you'll need to decide if that's the right path for you, but I want you to be able to make that choice, not have it made for you because you unknowingly went down the wrong path.

So let's consider you and where your career path is leading you. Would you get into a vehicle and let the driver decide where to take you? Of course not. However, I let this happen to me in my career. I let the company decide my path instead of determining my own. It's not that they didn't have my success in mind, but *they* decided what my success would look like, not me. Whose fault was that? No one but mine. I can't blame anyone but myself. If I had voiced my desire to become CEO early on, I know my career would have taken many different paths.

If getting to the CEO role at the end of the rainbow is your goal, let's make sure your career adventure takes you down the right path. Of course, whether you go down the right or wrong path depends on what you do for the next decade. Let's take a look at that now.

THE FIRST 10 YEARS: DEAD ENDS & POTS OF GOLD

I interviewed Greg Boyce, the former CEO of Peabody Energy (and one of the two CEOs I worked for), on an episode of *Preparing for the Possibility*, and we discussed how he had a wide variety of experiences by the time he became a CEO. He stated,

> "If you stay in a role until you are a 'Master of the Universe,' you are going to run out of time to get to CEO." [28]

He stressed that as a CEO, you ultimately rely on other people to be the experts. Value the experience and talent of the people working with you.

Since you're in the driver seat of your career, after a decade you'll have many experiences and have developed a strong foundation of skills and expertise, maybe all in one industry or maybe in multiple industries. You'll have likely mastered essential aspects in several disciplines, such as product development, business development, financial management, sales, marketing, and various aspects of operations. You'll be able to think and plan strategically, take strategic risks, and make decisions that align with long-term business objectives. You'll have been involved in setting company goals, planning for growth, and navigating challenges with a forward-thinking mindset. You'll have a track record of great results. Really fun stuff! What a fulfilling ten years this has been.

CORE SKILLS FOR MIDDLE MANAGEMENT

By the time you reach middle management, you'll have gotten some of the basics of leadership down. Becoming an effective leader is critical at this stage of your development, as honing the skills to manage others is essential. You'll be seeking opportunities in your organization that stretch your abilities, and by now, you'll be looking for a leadership role that involves either developing, creating, or selling your company's product or service.

And by now you'll be managing a team of people, a role that will be with you the rest of your career. Donna Brandin, a successful CFO in several organizations and board member for Nuveen Global, had this to say about her exposure to being a team leader:

> "When you start to manage people in your thirties, you really have to think about the team that surrounds you, not only how people supplement your strengths and weaknesses but also the strengths and weaknesses of the team." [29]

Many of us are moved into roles where a team already exists and we need to work with what we've got. But over time you'll be able to select your own team. Donna's message is a reminder that the best teams are not only composed of talented people individually but people who collectively are effective in what they do.

BASIC ADVICE FOR MIDDLE MANAGEMENT

Also at this point in your career, you'll need to understand the roles and responsibilities of a board of directors, the effective workings of an executive leadership team, and the impact your company's decisions have on key stakeholders. If your company has international operations, taking on a role in another country will not only offer you tremendous insights into the inner workings of your organization and to other countries' cultures, but it will also be highly valuable when you are considered for a CEO role in the future. International assignments are a great way to differentiate yourself from others who don't have that kind of experience.

REACHING THE FINISH LINE AND GETTING THE KEYS TO THE CASTLE

Pick up that CEO crystal ball again, ladies. After fifteen to twenty years in your career, you'll have held multiple high-level leadership roles. You'll have a long history of success with a track record of achieving business goals, driving revenue growth, and leading successful initiatives. Your accomplishments will be well-documented and recognized within the organization and industry. You'll possess deep insights into industry trends, competitive dynamics, and regulatory environments. You'll be sought after to speak about your industry. Your extensive knowledge will enable you to make informed decisions and provide valuable strategic direction. I'm impressed with how far you have come. Aren't you?

A PEEK AT YOU AS CEO

Now you'll either be seeking CEO opportunities with another organization that sees the impact you can make, becoming the head of the organization you are part of today, or maybe building a company of your own. After a decade of continuous education and expanding experiences, you'll finally be ready to take that step to becoming CEO.

At this stage, vision, leadership, strategic thinking and planning, and high-level decision-making skills become paramount. You'll be able to create and execute strategic visions. You'll have led long-term planning efforts, set organizational goals, and ensured cross-departmental alignment to achieve these objectives. You'll understand how effective staff organizations are critical to supporting the line and commercial sides of the business. You'll have successfully navigated your organization through significant changes, such as mergers, acquisitions, restructurings, and market shifts. Your experience in managing change has equipped you with the skills to handle complex transitions smoothly. As a CEO, you're now in a position to influence many things. Congratulations! You have a lot to be proud of!

And don't forget that by this time, you'll have a team of people following you. In an episode of *Preparing for the Possibility*, I spoke with Laura D'Asaro, the cofounder and CEO of Chirps, a food company seeking to transform dietary impact on the environment. We were discussing her journey to becoming a CEO, and she told me this:

> "What didn't come so easily, I think, was when you're CEO, you're thinking about your team members all the time It's not just about the vision, it's 'How are we functioning day-to-day? How do I help each of these people on my team grow?'" [30]

When your team knows this about you, they know they can trust you to take them to a better place. Never lose sight of this. Trust is an essential trait of being a successful leader.

How gratifying it is to glimpse into the crystal ball and see a future where possibilities become reality. But enough looking at the crystal ball. Let's get back to the reality of what you need to be doing right now.

CRAFT YOUR PERSONAL BRAND

Your personal brand is a summary of who you are and how others perceive you. We can look around and see leaders whose attributes consistently differentiate them from others. They're engaging and leave you feeling that they connected with you and you with them. These leaders have created their own personal brand that is unique to them. Take note: They are the movers and shakers in an organization.

Now, let's go to the beginning and discuss how they created their own personal brand.

To stand out in the crowd, you have to differentiate yourself from others. You have to have something about you that's unique. You can't just blend into the crowd alongside everyone else who's trying to succeed. First, there must be something about you that gets senior leaders to notice you. You need that special something, that secret sauce—a special blend of gumption and charisma.

Second, people need to want to follow you, not someone else, but you. And why you? Because they believe you know how to take them to the finish line. Remember, most leaders began with small teams of people, just as you'll have early in your career. But over time, as the size of your teams grows, so does your personal brand.

The previous chapters gave you a better understanding of the skills and traits of a successful CEO. Now it's time to make your mark. In other words, develop your own personal brand of who you are as a leader. I've outlined four steps below to get you thinking about crafting a personal brand that others will notice. But first, I want to talk a little more about the importance of a personal brand.

Your personal brand is your professional persona's heartbeat. It's what people say about you when you're not in the room, and it's your vibe that attracts opportunities.

Your personal brand is like your signature—unique, distinctive, and a statement of who you are and what you stand for in the professional world. It's your story, your values, and your vision, all rolled into one compelling package that resonates with people even before you enter the room.

As we discussed earlier, some leaders are known for their creativity, some for their charisma, some for their work ethic, some for their intellect, some for their courage, some for their compassion, some for their resilience, some for their confidence, and the list goes on. And many great leaders combine these traits, giving them a very distinctive personal brand.

A strong personal brand isn't an option; it's a must. Here's why:

- **Visibility:** In a world buzzing with talent, your personal brand helps you stand out and positions you as a thought-leader and impact-maker.
- **Credibility:** A strong personal brand builds trust. People are more likely to believe in you—and by extension, in your leadership—when they know what you stand for. Trust and successful leadership go hand in hand.
- **Career accelerator:** Your personal brand is a magnet for opportunities. A powerful personal brand attracts the right people at the right moments, propelling your career forward. In other words, it helps you make your own luck.

We've all heard this, but what the Roman philosopher Seneca wrote bears repeating: "Luck is what happens when preparation meets opportunity." What this means for you is that the more you can do to make yourself valuable to a team, the luckier you'll become in accelerating your career. I found this to be true for many successful people I met over my years, not only in business but in life in general. Preparation and luck go hand in hand.

I talked to Pooneh Mohajer, the cofounder and CEO of tokidoki, on an episode of *Preparing for the Possibility*, and she offered some great advice on making a difference. In regards to her own growth, she said:

> "I'm not saying you have to work every Sunday, but it's going above and beyond the basic requirements of your job; it's taking your passion to another level and showing up for yourself. Others will notice, and it's not just for yourself; you're really showing up for the greater good, the organization, whatever team you're on. You're showing up for your colleagues." [31]

So now that you're on a path to creating your own personal brand, how do you ensure your personal brand is visible and reflects the mark you're making?

The **first step in** creating your own personal brand is to visualize how you'll differentiate yourself.

When I began my career in the early 1980s, it was uncommon for women to have an MBA. Even men having an MBA was a mark of distinction. In my early twenties, I decided I needed to differentiate myself from others and went to night school to complete an MBA. I believe that this credential influenced not only how I approached business but how my company's senior management viewed me.

In other words, it got me noticed.

I'm not telling you to get an advanced degree, but I am suggesting that you differentiate yourself from the masses. Think this through and come up with something that's right for you and will benefit others.

Step two: Be consistent. Whether it's your presence in the office or online, the quality of your professional interactions, work ethic, and consistency in how you present yourself reinforce your brand identity. This is especially true when you're networking within your company or within your industry.

In an episode of *Preparing for the Possibility,* I interviewed Lauren Evans, the president, CEO, and chair of Pinyon Environmental. She told me,

> "You have to build a network . . . a network of people you trust and who trust you."[32]

A network like that happens over time, but the key is to start building it early in your career.

Your brand grows in value when you engage and connect with others within your organization, industry, and in other industries. When you attend seminars, connect with others and stay in contact with them. For example, if you read they've been promoted, drop them a note to congratulate them. You never know how those relationships might help you in the future.

Step three: Share your story—your journey, challenges, victories, and learnings. People connect with stories, and it makes your brand relatable and memorable.

Ask others to share their stories, too. People are flattered when you ask them to talk about themselves, and you might learn something from them as well.

Step four can be the most difficult for some. Stay open to feedback about how others perceive your brand. It's a goldmine for refining and evolving your brand strategy, so don't avoid it. Crafting your personal brand isn't a singular event. It's a journey of self-discovery, storytelling, and strategic positioning that sets the stage for your ascent to CEO. We likely all know people who seemed to have everything going for them only to have one important issue hold them back from reaching greater heights. Unfortunately, learning from feedback wasn't a card they wanted to play, and in the end, it cost them the game.

Let your personal brand be the constant that ties your experiences together, showcasing your unique leadership style and vision.

Are you ready to create a brand that stands out from the crowd, echoes your aspirations, and shows the mark you're making in your industry and beyond?

STEP UP AND MAKE AN IMPACT

Transforming from a team player to a team leader is like stepping out of the wings and into the spotlight. It's about evolving into someone who makes things happen, guiding their squad with a vision and a rock-solid strategy. Be the person others want to be around.

Dive into roles and opportunities that flex your leadership muscles and allow you to rally others toward a shared goal. Lead volunteer groups or work with your manager to start a project that lights you up.

You're not just aiming to be any leader; you're on the path to becoming an impactful CEO. This journey is about blending your unique talents with smart, strategic moves. It's about grabbing every chance to learn, grow, and, ultimately, stand out.

Your mission is to lead in such a groundbreaking way that people can't help but follow you. Keep your eyes on the prize, and remember, every challenge you face is another opportunity to prove you've got what it takes to make it to the top.

So let's get moving! Make your mark and show the world the kind of CEO you're destined to become.

Now that you understand how to craft a personal brand that stands out from the crowd, the next step of your CEO journey is to decide who you want by your side along the way. Up next, we'll talk about how to build your personal board of directors.

ABC CALLOUTS

Here's a quick rundown of the ABC's for making your mark:

A. **Aspire to lead with more than ambition:** It's about making an impact that echoes. You need to become the person whose performance always exceeds your goals.

B. **Build a strong foundation:** Embrace essential skills and effective leadership traits. Continuously learning will lay the groundwork for innovative leadership. Tailor your journey with experiences that align with your aspirations and expand your horizons.

C. **Craft your signature brand:** Establishing a consistent and effective personal brand—or your professional persona—is key to attracting attention and showcasing your unique leadership style, vibe, and vision.

CEO

INSIGHT

"Find the smartest people you can and surround yourself with them."

———

—Marissa Mayer, former President and CEO of Yahoo

Chapter 6

CURATE YOUR CIRCLE
SURROUND YOURSELF WITH VISIONARIES, SUPPORTERS, AND THOSE WHO WILL BE HONEST WITH YOU

C an you imagine a circle of mentors, supporters, promoters, and business coaches, each adding their unique blend of wisdom, experience, and encouragement to your leadership journey? If you can imagine it, you can create it!

We're going to call this group your personal board of directors. This isn't just a nice idea—it's a game-changer, and it's extremely beneficial in making that climb to the CEO chair. It's like having an all-star team, where everyone plays a crucial role in guiding you through ups and downs, celebrating your wins, motivating you during setbacks, keeping you grounded and focused on your goal, and providing you with meaningful feedback.

In this chapter, I'll show you how to craft this invaluable support system and share insights and actionable strategies.

ASSEMBLE YOUR DREAM TEAM

Assembling your board of directors is more than just selecting people willy-nilly. Your board should rock as much as you do.

If there's ever a time to treat yourself, it's now.

Building your personal board is about curating a group of individuals who bring diverse perspectives, skills, and experiences to the table. And, by the way, as you evolve over time, your board will likely evolve, too.

Think of it as putting together a successful band. Every member plays a different instrument, and everyone contributes to creating hit songs—your career success. What's essential here is a mix of guidance, challenges, coaching, tough love, and, yes, a bit of cheerleading, too.

But this crew isn't just cheering you on from the sidelines; they're in the game *with* you, offering wisdom and support every step of the way.

And while it's cool to have industry giants in your corner, don't overlook the hidden gems. Consider talking to your past teachers or professors, former coworkers, prior coaches, and other insightful family or friends. Their with unique insights who can really add depth to your growth.

Your team should include lots of mentors, supporters, and promoters. Consider hiring a personal coach, as well. They're a valuable resource so long as you can afford their services.

MENTOR(S)

A good business mentor should know the ins and outs of business in general, help you network, teach you what you can't learn on your own, and give you honest advice and tough love.

A good aspirational mentor is someone who encourages you to go the distance, celebrates with you when times are good, and inspires you when you're feeling down. This individual may or may not be familiar with your business, specifically.

Generally, a mentor is someone you can connect with, a trustworthy person you can confide in.

When you start a new job, many companies will pair you with a business mentor. Hopefully, your mentor matches what we've described here. But if you're not clicking with your assigned mentor, don't immediately start asking to switch. Give your first mentor some time before looking for a new one. You don't want to alienate someone who could be a valuable ally in the future.

Having multiple mentors is a real plus. Seek out some mentors who aren't a part of your organization. These are typically people who have been there and done that, either in your industry or in another. Having mentors outside of your industry can provide you with fresh perspectives on business issues. These types of mentors are vital, particularly if you ever consider moving to another organization or industry.

SUPPORTER(S)

A supporter is someone who sits at the organization's talent management meetings and actively participates in succession planning. A supporter can "put your name on the table" during these discussions. It's important to meet periodically with supporters to keep them posted on your career goals and your thoughts on assignments that might help you achieve those goals.

Unlike mentors, you typically don't formally ask others to be a supporter. Instead, you build a relationship with them that allows you to communicate your career goals so they can support you.

In an interview I did with Cabanne Howard, the founder and CEO of Kaleidoscope Management Group, she said:

> "Don't be afraid to ask for or say what you want. Women
> tend to shy away from what they want because they may
> be perceived as being too greedy." [33]

Remember, you're in the driver seat when it comes to your career path. Clearly communicating where you want to go isn't being greedy—it's standing up for yourself.

If you're new to your organization, it may take some time to evaluate who are the players (i.e., the supporters) you need to know and who needs to know *you* and your aspirations.

PROMOTER(S)

These are the people who have seen you in action . . . and *loved* it. They can directly speak to your contributions to projects and the teams you've been part of. These are the individuals who sing your praises.

Letting promoters know that you're interested in working with them on other projects is important because *you* will continue to shine, and *they* will continue to have positive things to say about you.

As with supporters, you don't formally ask someone to be a promoter; they naturally become one by observing your contributions and potential. Having many promoters is a bonus because word about your contributions will spread more quickly.

PERSONAL COACH(ES)

A personal coach is a thinking partner who helps you develop and grow as a leader. They'll help you develop your leadership skills to more effectively interact and collaborate with others.

Coaches will often give you assessments, which can provide actionable insights about your strengths and developmental needs. Some organizations will provide this type of testing to employees, but I've found that organizations don't always provide this resource until you reach a certain level of management, which is unfortunate. Early intervention regarding your developmental needs can be more effective than waiting until you're already several years into your career.

For example, a person who starts learning a sport at an early age will be better at that sport than someone who started later in life. I enjoy playing golf; what I would give now to have had lessons when I was younger. The same can be said for becoming a leader. Changing bad habits is difficult, while learning the right skills at an early age makes for a better golfer and a better leader.

I know several CEOs who use coaches. I've heard that being a CEO is somewhat lonely, so it helps to have another person to confide in. Some coaches can help you think through complex business issues, while others are sounding boards to discuss management issues. Whatever the reason, coaches can be valuable resources.

If your company offers you a coach, go for it. If not, research finding one on your own. You might even hint to someone that sessions with a coach would be a nice gift to receive!

BUILD YOUR SQUAD

It's tempting to think that one seasoned mentor, someone who's been there and done that, could be your only guiding voice, but as I mentioned earlier, I suggest having more than one mentor . . . *and* I suggest having a few outside of your professional network.

Remember, treat yourself to this opportunity.

What if I told you that in addition to several seasoned mentors, your community of friends and acquaintances can be just as powerful? This isn't about finding a mentor in the traditional sense—it's about surrounding yourself with people who share your passion, drive, and vision. It might be an aunt, uncle, or a family friend. You might find someone in your network of friends who is willing to be part of your journey. Don't limit yourself to people in your work environment.

Picture your support network as a vibrant group chat where every participant brings something valuable to the conversation—a conversation where the goal isn't necessarily consensus but in letting ideas flow freely.

Imagine doing this with your dream squad. Here are some general guidelines to finding the right people.

STEP 1: PINPOINT YOUR GOALS

Get crystal clear on what you want.

What are the big wins—your lofty goals for your career—both now and down the road?

Formulating these goals helps you figure out exactly who you need in your corner and what you need to articulate to your personal board of directors about your desired career path. If you're struggling with defining your goals, talk to your mentor and ask for their insights.

Sometimes, after you meet with potential mentors, you may need to consider new ideas to further pinpoint your goals. Remember, in the face of new and relevant information, flexibility is a trait of a good leader. Don't be afraid to revise your goals.

STEP 2: IDENTIFY YOUR NEEDS
Look at where you're heading and ask yourself, "What expertise do I need to get there?" Maybe it's a marketing maven, a proven negotiator, or a finance whiz. Knowing what skills and experience you need is key to selecting your mentors. As your skills evolve, you'll want to consider new or additional mentors to help expand your expertise.

STEP 3: SCOUT FOR TALENT
Keep your eyes peeled for potential champions both inside and outside of your organization. Networking events, industry conferences, and even online networks can be gold mines for finding individuals who align with your vision and goals.

Scout for leaders who have a reputation for being change agents. These people have insights into business "politics" (yes, there's politics outside of the government) and have often excelled in cross-functional roles. They can inspire bold moves, offer holistic views, and provide invaluable leadership advice. This will help you develop a more inclusive and adaptable leadership style.

When you're looking for champions to support your career path, aim for a variety of backgrounds. Creating a personal board of directors with diverse perspectives will give you insight from various industries and different cultural backgrounds, enriching your leadership journey. Diversity helps you navigate complex challenges while showing you where your blind spots are.

STEP 4: REACH OUT

Now for the fun part—making the connection. In an episode of *Preparing for the Possibility* I did with Julie Lilly, the CEO of St. Louis Trust, she stated,

"Opportunity often finds you through relationships." [34]

You never know where a connection might take you. And when you connect, be genuine. Share your vision, why you admire them, and how you think they could help you blaze your trail to the top. Consider how you can help them in return.

STEP 5: NURTURE THE RELATIONSHIP

It's not just about making the offer. It's about building a real two-way relationship. Remember, a healthy relationship isn't just about you. Respect your mentors' time and come prepared for your meetings. Keep them updated on your progress, ask for advice when you need it, and always show your appreciation.

Building your personal board of directors is more than just rounding up a group of mentors. It's about creating a powerhouse team. With the right people by your side, the path to CEO gets a little clearer.

ENGAGE YOUR DREAM TEAM AND FOSTER DYNAMIC BONDS

Now that you've got the right people at the table, it's time to engage them.

Engaging your dream team is crucial because it lets you tap into the full potential of your personal board of directors. By actively seeking input, advice, and feedback from a range of advisors, you can more deeply understand the challenges and opportunities leaders face. Engagement also fosters a sense of shared purpose.

So how do you manage this awesome squad of mentors and advisors ready to help catapult you to success? Let's get into the details of connecting with your personal board of directors:

- **Schedule regular chats:** Regularly schedule one-on-one catch-up time. These aren't just any meetings; they're your chance to open up about where you're at, the bumps you're hitting, and the wins you're celebrating. Keeping it consistent shows you're serious and value their input. By the way, coffee or lunch is always on you!

- **Lay your cards on the table**: Be upfront about your big dreams and how you want your mentors to help you. Sharing your blueprint makes them feel like true copilots on your professional journey.

- **Ask for their "secret sauce":** Everyone's got their strong suits, right? By seeking advice that plays to your mentor's strengths, you're not just getting gold, you're also showing you've done your homework and value what they bring to the table. But be genuine; these are smart people you're inviting onto your personal board. Don't give them false compliments, or they'll think you're patronizing them.

- **Circle back with the deets:** After your mentor has dropped some wisdom, let them know what happened when you followed their advice. Sharing how you implemented their ideas shows you respect and appreciate their guidance.

- **Make it a two-way street:** Flip the script and bring value to the table for them. Whether it's a fresh perspective, a resource you've found invaluable, or a new challenge you can tackle together, reciprocity keeps the relationship dynamic and mutually enriching.

- **Don't skimp on the thank yous:** A little gratitude goes a long way. Acknowledge the role they're playing in your climb. Building a culture of appreciation will help keep them engaged.

By following these steps, you'll not only strengthen your connections with your mentors but also create a supportive network that will be there for you every step of the way. So go ahead! Foster those dynamic bonds and watch your career soar to new heights!

EXPAND YOUR NETWORK HORIZONS

Your board's encouragement, sound advice, and actionable wisdom will propel you forward. When you follow these steps, you're not just building a board, you're crafting a dream team of mentors who are as invested in your journey as you are. Every CEO should have a diverse group of advisers on their company's board of directors, and every aspiring leader should thoughtfully build a dynamic *personal* board filled with people whose experiences and expertise challenge and inspire them to reach new heights.

Each step, from recognizing the value of mentors to expanding your mentorship horizons, is another strategic move toward your career goals. By cultivating a supportive and dynamic network, you're not only preparing for leadership roles, you're also laying the groundwork for visionary and transformative leadership skills that will guide you to the pinnacle of professional achievement—becoming a CEO.

With the right people by your side, the path to CEO becomes clearer and more attainable. Let's get to it!

ABC CALLOUTS

Alright, let's sum this up with the essentials for creating and bonding with your personal board of directors, particularly your mentor:

A. **Assemble your circle:** Look for mentors and business coaches who will guide you on your journey to becoming a CEO. Think of where you need expertise the most. Alongside mentors and coaches, make sure your supporters and promoters within the company know about your long-term objective of becoming a CEO.

B. **Broaden your horizons:** Look for several mentors both inside and outside of your industry. Expand your mentorship circle to include voices from different industries, backgrounds, and experiences to gain a well-rounded perspective on leadership. An aspirational mentor will be invaluable as you navigate the ups and downs of your career journey. Surround yourself with people who want to see you succeed.

C. **Cement relationships:** Nurture these bonds. Invest time and energy into building strong connections with your board through regular, meaningful interactions. Share your dreams, seek their wisdom, and update them on your progress. Remember, gratitude goes a long way.

CEO
INSIGHT

"If you can let go of passion and follow your curiosity, your curiosity just might lead you to your passion."

———

—Elizabeth Gilbert, author

Chapter 7

BECOME CURIOUS
COMMIT TO YOUR GROWTH AND ADAPTATION

You may be thinking, "I don't have a passion to be a CEO, so why should I set my sights on it?" But aren't you curious—even just a little—about why someone might be passionate about it?

Most people who become CEOs started where you may be today . . . one of many new employees who are eager to prove themselves. But becoming a CEO isn't like becoming an engineer, an architect, an accountant, a lawyer, or any other career path that focuses on a specific set of skills. A CEO may start there, but it's not where their journey ends.

Becoming a CEO requires constantly learning and developing diverse skills.

Do you know that feeling of being a beginner and the path to competence—not to mention excellence—seems like a huge mountain to climb?

That's what it can feel like for someone early in their career even thinking about becoming CEO. That goal can feel impossible. Maybe you don't even realize now that you might want it someday.

LIFELONG LEARNING

Here's a truth bomb: If you're an aspiring leader, NEVER stop learning, even though you'll never know everything there is to know.

In our fast-paced world, the ultimate competitive edge lies in your ability to continuously learn. This includes accepting failure and learning to adapt.

Your success depends on your eagerness to embrace new knowledge, challenge the status quo, and stay ahead of the curve.

Continuous learning is nonnegotiable. The business landscape is evolving at lightning speed, making yesterday's best practices obsolete. To stay relevant and effective, you need a mindset of lifelong learning.

The journey to the top is paved with lessons, some you'll actively seek out and others that will find you. The mark of a great leader isn't how many titles or accomplishments they've collected. It's their ability to grow and evolve over time that sets them apart.

The world changes, industries evolve, and new challenges pop up when you least expect them. Staying informed and open to learning is what will set you apart.

But an effective leader needs more than knowledge. They're curious. They're tenacious. They push the boundaries. So how do you cultivate this superpower?

First, view every experience as a learning opportunity. *Especially* the failures.

Mistakes are rich with insights if you're willing to dissect them.

Next, stay curious about your field of expertise and keep an eye on the horizon for changes in the status quo. The broader your knowledge base, the more innovative your solutions will be. Always surround yourself with others who know more than you. Attend conferences, read voraciously, and never shy away from asking questions, no matter how basic they may seem.

I had a colleague once who believed that asking questions was a sign of weakness, while another colleague believed that thoughtful questions led to more knowledge. When they were in meetings together, the former always tried to give the impression he understood everything and that he already knew all of the information being presented. The latter was continuously engaged in the meeting and asked meaningful questions, including many I wished I'd thought of myself.

Fast-forward ten years after first meeting these colleagues. The "know-it-all" colleague never made it past being a manager. The other became a senior executive. The lesson here is to never hesitate to ask thoughtful questions when you're learning something. It's not a sign of weakness.

One last point about learning: Regardless of your achievements, always embrace a student's mindset. There's always something new to learn, a different perspective to consider, or a skill to refine.

I once did an episode of *Preparing for the Possibility* with Ward Klein, the former CEO of Energizer, and he had a great statement about learning. He said:

"You learn more when you listen than when you talk." [35]

A lesson for us in business and in life.

The CEO chair requires more than just experience; it demands a leader who knows their strengths and weaknesses and is continually evolving. By committing to lifelong learning, you're gearing up to lead an industry (or even multiple industries) and make an impact that resonates beyond your tenure. A successful person surrounds themself with individuals who can bring to the table the expertise that they lack. Never forget that knowing your weaknesses is as important as knowing your strengths.

In the quest to become a CEO, your greatest asset isn't just your resume; it's your willingness to grow and adapt. So keep learning, keep challenging yourself, and let the journey transform you into the leader you can become.

MAKE LEARNING A DAILY HABIT

As I began to consider when it would be time for me to become "post-career" (i.e., retire), I asked a CEO friend of mine for his advice on knowing when it's the right time. He said that when you begin solving the same problem over and over without coming up with a new solution, it's time to make a change. I'm not sure I ever got to that stage, but the point is that as long as you keep learning something new, you can continue to make a difference.

Turning learning into a daily habit is hard work. Doing something on a regular, consistent basis requires discipline.

You have to make learning a daily habit, but reading publications or taking classes aren't your only options. Here are a few ideas you can use to cultivate a culture of continuous learning in your career:

- Actively engaging in meetings
- Asking colleagues and others thoughtful questions

- Taking on challenging assignments
- Seeking out mentors and role models who can impart their wisdom

But don't limit yourself to your own industry—seek inspiration and insights beyond your borders.

BE CURIOUS

Did curiosity really *kill* the cat?

Hmmmm . . . let's think about this.

How many great inventions and innovations happened because someone wondered how to make something better? How many breakthroughs in science and technology were accidental because someone was curious? How many times has cultural norms changed because someone believed there was a better way of treating people? Over the years, curiosity has led to many important discoveries.

In an interview I did with Barbara Archer, the founder and former president of Archer Wealth Management, we discussed learning, and she made a great statement regarding curiosity:

"Do not let people put limitations on your own curiosity." [36]

The moral here is to be as curious as you want! Don't let "Curiosity killed the cat" be your mantra!

Without curiosity, we stand still. A life without curiosity is stagnant—and that's not a good thing for anyone. Without the desire to learn and grow, creating a better path forward is difficult if not impossible. Understanding different perspectives, what makes people tick, and how to make things better are all positive motivations. Not everything needs to be life-changing. Simply making a daily activity more efficient is learning.

Explore your curiosities. You may be amazed at the path it takes you down.

IT'S OK TO FAIL

Finally, don't be afraid to take risks in your career. Some of the most rewarding detours involve a leap of faith—be willing to try something new, especially if it's uncertain and failure is a possible outcome. Embracing failure is a catalyst for growth. Failure isn't something to fear; if you learn from a failure, it's a teacher.

Every setback, misstep, and disappointment are chances to learn and come back stronger. Of course, if you're experiencing more failures than successes over time, you may need to step back and re-evaluate your decision-making process and your risk-taking skills.

Have the courage to take risks, try new approaches, and learn valuable lessons from your failures.

PIVOT AND RECALIBRATE

Adaptability is a critical trait for lifelong learners. The ability to pivot, recalibrate, and move forward again to navigate uncharted territory is key. Stay open to new opportunities, even if they don't fit your original plan. Be willing to let go of what's not working and try new strategies. Cultivate the resilience to thrive in any situation.

Risk-taking and adaptability require skills and an intentional mindset. As with anything new you learn, start with small steps. Remember what we discussed in Chapter 4: Taking risks takes practice, and it often doesn't feel natural.

That bears repeating. Taking risks early in your career could mean challenging an idea that someone brings up in a meeting, suggesting ways to improve your department's processes, or applying for a stretch assignment or a different position that will require new skills and competencies.

Approach your career and life with openness, curiosity, and a commitment to growth and continuous learning. As a future CEO, these qualities are your ticket to reaching your full potential and making a lasting impact.

So keep learning. Keep evolving. And don't shy away from change. It's the leaders who embrace these attributes who come out on top. And isn't that your goal?

ABC CALLOUTS

Let's recap the essential ABC's for navigating your career journey:

A. **Adopt a growth mindset:** Make self-development a daily habit. Invest in continuous learning to expand your skills and gain new experiences.

B. **Behind every setback is an opportunity:** Transform detours into opportunities. View career diversions as chances for growth and discovery. Welcome change and discomfort as catalysts for personal and professional development.

C. **Curiosity, risk taking, and adaptability are key:** Get outside your comfort zone to stay relevant and effective in an ever-evolving business landscape. Failure is not the enemy—it's a teacher, if you allow it to be.

CEO INSIGHT

"Feedback is a free education to excellence. Seek it with sincerity and receive it with grace."

———

—Ann marie Houghtailing, Cofounder
and CEO of Story Imprinting

Chapter 8

EMBRACE INSIGHTS
TRANSFORM CRITICISM INTO YOUR LEADERSHIP FUEL

Do you like getting feedback? Do you dread it as a necessary evil, or do you welcome it?

Love it, hate it, or fear it, the right feedback can supercharge your leadership journey. Even if it makes you uncomfortable, feedback is a career vitamin that will build you into a stronger leader and accelerate your journey to the role of CEO.

Genuine feedback is like a mirror, reflecting how others perceive your actions and leadership style. It can illuminate your strengths, highlight your blind spots, and provide a roadmap for growth and refinement. When you create a culture of open feedback within your team, you unlock the possibility for continuous improvement.

Seeking and receiving feedback requires being vulnerable and willing to confront uncomfortable truths about ourselves. But the leaders who rise to the top are the ones who embrace that discomfort, seeing feedback as an opportunity to learn and improve. Let's explore the art and science of seeking feedback and how to maximize what we learn from it. You'll learn some strategies for soliciting feedback and distinguishing between constructive criticism and less beneficial feedback.

NOT ALL FEEDBACK FEELS GOOD

By definition, good leaders are successful because they embody many positive characteristics. However, good leaders also recognize that they aren't perfect and accept constructive feedback and suggestions as opportunities to make their leadership more effective.

Constructive feedback has become somewhat of a polite cliché for advice regarding areas of improvement. Effective constructive feedback is specific, actionable, and diplomatic. The intent is to help you grow and improve. Constructive feedback illuminates areas where you have room to develop and provides guidance on how to get there.

Great leaders understand that growth and comfort rarely coexist and that the path to excellent leadership is paved with moments of discomfort and self-reflection.

As a new leader, you must embrace constructive feedback. Proactively seek it out from trusted mentors, colleagues, and your team. You can even get 360-degree feedback from stakeholders. Look for criticism that is relevant and respectful.

Unfortunately, not everyone who provides feedback has been trained on the most effective way to deliver it. In your career, you'll likely receive feedback that doesn't seem like it was intended to help you grow. Instead, it leaves you feeling down. Part of your growth opportunity will be to learn how to move forward in a positive way despite the negative feedback. Look beyond the negativity and focus on the valuable message that you can walk away with.

Embracing constructive feedback is difficult but worthwhile. By leaning into feedback with an open mind and a growth mindset, you'll unlock new insights about yourself that can propel you toward leadership greatness.

In a discussion I had with Marcela Manjarrez, the CEO of M Strategic Communications Consulting and author of *The CEO's Competitive Advantage*, she said:

> "There is no such thing as a mistake, every challenge you face is an opportunity for growth and development. Don't be afraid to ask for opportunities. No matter the outcome, what you learn along the way will set you up for success." [37]

No matter the company, sometimes things just go wrong. It's inevitable. As a result, CEOs often have to deal with negative reactions from stakeholders. Sometimes the criticism is justified, while other times, CEOs have to figure out how to deal with stakeholders who are just plain wrong about a situation. A CEO who knows how to productively address the situation with grace and poise can keep it from escalating. So remember, handling negative feedback is also part of the training for becoming a CEO!

ACTIVELY SOLICIT

To truly accelerate your growth and reach your full potential, pro-actively seek out feedback. Become someone who actively encourages feedback.

Start by identifying key stakeholders in your professional sphere who have a vested interest in your success and can offer valuable insights. This might include your boss, peers, subordinates, and even external stakeholders like customers or clients.

Approach feedback conversations with curiosity and openness, making it clear that you value the other person's perspective and are committed to considering their feedback to grow and improve.

Make it abundantly clear that they can share their honest perspectives without fear of retribution or judgment. Actively listen to feedback, even when it's surprising or difficult to hear, and, above all, don't become defensive. Listen and appreciate the courage and vulnerability it takes to offer constructive criticism.

Once you receive feedback, take the time to reflect on it and identify patterns and themes. If it's an important issue, develop a plan to address it. Be willing to have difficult conversations and make tough choices, whether that means admitting when you've made a mistake or making changes to your leadership style or approach. A healthy dose of humility can go a long way here. You won't always agree with feedback, and whether you want to act on that feedback is ultimately your call. But beware, if the same feedback comes up multiple times from different sources, pay attention. It could potentially be a blind spot and a roadblock to reaching your ultimate goal.

Start the conversation and let the feedback flow. Ask open ended questions; let others know they're doing you a favor when they give you honest feedback; ask for details and further explanations; let the other person know you appreciate their guidance; and, finally, if the feedback is useful, consider how you'll act on it. Implementing feedback can take days, weeks, or sometimes months. The point is to not lose sight of it.

Whenever someone gives you constructive feedback, they'll likely balance it with positive feedback. Don't make light of positive feedback. Accept the praise gracefully!

ANALYZE AND APPLY

Alright, future CEO, you've actively solicited feedback and embraced constructive criticism. Now what?

It's time to take that valuable input and turn it into tangible growth and improvement.

Analyzing feedback effectively is all about unearthing the actionable insights hidden within. You have to listen and dig for the underlying message and identify the key takeaways to drive your development forward.

One extremely effective method for analyzing feedback is to look for patterns and themes.

Are there certain areas that come up repeatedly, either as strengths or weaknesses? If so, listen closely! These patterns can help you prioritize your growth efforts and focus on the issues that will have the biggest impact on your leadership.

For example, have you heard multiple times that you need to listen more and talk less, that you come across as finding "the glass half empty" too often, that you alienate others in how you approach solving a problem, or that you don't check your work product thoroughly before handing it off? If you've heard the same feedback more than once, you need to get serious about changing this pattern of behavior.

Another key strategy is to ask clarifying questions and seek specific examples. If someone's feedback feels vague or unclear, dig deeper. Ask for concrete examples of the behavior in question or request suggestions on how you could handle similar situations differently in the future.

The more specific and actionable the feedback, the more useful it will be in driving your growth.

Remember, when someone gives you feedback and you feel disappointed by their observation, you can't take it personally. Too often I find that women will let negative feedback kill their self-confidence. If the feedback is valid, treat it as an opportunity to get it right the next time. If the feedback is invalid, you can state why you believe it's wrong, but don't get defensive and argue about it. And if you hear the same feedback on another occasion, take a moment to step back and determine if you have a blind spot that you need to pay attention to.

On the other hand, I have also found that too many women don't take compliments seriously. If someone tells you that you did a good job, accept it and say, "Thank you!" Yes, it may be true that you were part of a team working together, and it's OK if you also want to acknowledge them, but don't take the spotlight totally off of yourself.

Once you've analyzed the feedback and identified the key insights, it's time to put them into action. This is where developing a systematic approach to incorporating feedback into your personal development plan comes in.

One effective framework is to create a feedback loop: Set specific, measurable goals based on your feedback, develop a plan to achieve those goals, track your progress over time, seek out more feedback to assess your improvement, and identify new areas for growth.

By making feedback a regular and ongoing part of your development process, you can ensure that you're always moving forward and pushing yourself to new heights.

Of course, implementing feedback is usually the harder part. It's challenging to face our weaknesses head-on and change our behavior and leadership style. But remember, discomfort is often a sign of growth. By embracing the challenges and pushing yourself outside your comfort zone, you'll emerge a stronger, more effective leader on the other side.

If you've been coached to listen more when others are speaking, make it a point to ask a question or affirm something they said. If your feedback says you're too cynical, pause before stating your perspective on something and incorporate a positive comment. If you're making too many mistakes in your work product, take the time to double check your work before passing it on. Feedback is supposed to change your behavior, not simply be set aside once you get it. To make the most of it, you need to use it.

ADDRESS PERFORMANCE GAPS

No matter how talented or experienced you are, there will always be areas where you can improve as a leader. The key is to proactively identify those performance gaps and develop targeted strategies to address them head-on.

This is where feedback is an invaluable tool. By seeking out honest, constructive input from a variety of sources, you can gain a clearer picture of where you excel and where you have room for growth. The key is to approach this process with an open mind and a willingness to face your weaknesses directly.

In an episode of *Preparing for the Possibility* I did with Lisa Nichols, the cofounder and CEO of Technology Partners, she told me:

> "I'm a big believer in working from your strength zones and having the humility to say 'I'm not very good at that, so I need to lean in to someone else.'" [38]

I can't repeat this enough, never be intimidated to have someone on your team who knows something better than you do.

Once you've identified your performance gaps, it's time to craft a detailed action plan to address them. This plan should be specific, measurable, and time-bound, with clear milestones and checkpoints along the way to help you track your progress.

For example, let's say you've been asked to lead a team on a project, and you know from previous feedback that you struggle with delegating tasks effectively. Your action plan might include steps like these:

1. Assess your current delegation habits and identify the root causes of your reluctance to delegate (e.g., fear of losing control, lack of trust in your team, believing you can do it better and faster yourself, etc.).

2. Develop a list of delegatable tasks and responsibilities and identify team members who have the skills and expertise to take them on.

3. Set up regular check-ins with your team to provide guidance and support as they take on new responsibilities.

4. Seek out opportunities to practice delegation in low-risk

situations, gradually building up to more complex and high-stakes tasks.

5. Solicit feedback from your supervisor and your team on your delegation skills and use that input to continue refining your approach over time.

By breaking down your performance gaps into specific, actionable steps, you can make steady progress toward becoming a more well-rounded, effective leader.

CULTIVATE CONTINUOUS IMPROVEMENT

Becoming a great leader isn't a one-time event—it's a lifelong journey of learning, growth, and continuous improvement. And one of the most powerful fuels for that journey is a steady stream of honest, constructive feedback.

Ultimately, cultivating continuous improvement is about recognizing that leadership is a journey, not a destination. We should always be learning, growing, and pushing ourselves to new heights.

By making feedback a regular and integral part of that journey, you'll accelerate your own growth as a leader and inspire others to do the same.

A savvy CEO knows that continuous improvement is never done—for the company or themselves. There are always new avenues to explore and new mountains to climb. Let's start exploring and climbing now!

ABC CALLOUTS

Feedback is a crucial tool for leadership development. Let's recap the essential ABC's for seeking feedback:

A. **Actively solicit feedback:** Ask your supervisors, peers, subordinates, and stakeholders for their input. The more perspectives you have, the more opportunities you have for growth. Analyze the feedback to identify patterns, themes, and actionable insights.

B. **Be open to constructive feedback:** Don't take constructive criticism personally. Keep an open mind and be willing to learn and improve.

C. **Craft detailed action plans:** Use your feedback to build new skills, overcome weaknesses, and address performance gaps head-on. And don't forget to pat yourself on the back for a job well-done!

CEO
INSIGHT

"You can break that big plan into small steps and take the first step right away."

———

—Indira Gandhi, former Prime Minister of India

Chapter 9

MAP YOUR IMPACT
STRATEGIZE WITH PURPOSE, EXECUTE WITH PASSION

What career path would you choose if you had no fear?

When you're early in your career, thinking about becoming a CEO may seem a little unrealistic and, quite honestly, maybe even a little scary. But you don't just decide "I'm going to be a CEO" and then it happens. As we've discussed, it's a process, and the right preparation will make it more likely—and a lot less scary. Like an Olympic gold medalist, success comes with desire and preparation . . . and linking that preparation to your natural talents.

You now understand that there isn't one "right" path to becoming a CEO; there are multiple. But there are also dead-end paths.

Actually, there are probably as many different paths as there are CEOs, each unique to the individual. That means you can and should chart a course that feels authentic to who you are and aligns with your unique strengths, passions, values, and aspirations.

So what does your right path look like? It's the one that leverages your strengths, challenges you to grow, feeds off of your values, ignites your passion, and feels natural to you. It's the path that feels like a thrilling adventure, even on the toughest days.

Remember, your leadership journey is a marathon, not a sprint. And in this marathon, you get to design the route, set the pace, and decide where the finish line is. It's understanding the roadblocks to avoid and finding a path that works for you.

When I first had the idea to found my organization, ABC to CEO, I kept envisioning a maze, one with plenty of dead ends but also a number of paths that lead to the goal. (In fact, our logo has a maze in it!) I suspect that most CEOs would describe their journey as a path that was fraught with obstacles, and yours will likely be similar. Realize that facing obstacles is to be expected, not a message for you to give up. It simply means that your path, although unique to you, will be filled with hurdles that you can manage.

Embrace the opportunity to plot your one-of-a-kind path to the top. When you lead with authenticity and purpose, there's no limit to how high you can soar.

IDENTIFY YOUR UNIQUE STRENGTHS AND VALUES

As we already reviewed in Chapter 4, before embarking on your leadership journey, you need to know what makes you tick. This means recognizing your personal strengths and values—the qualities that set you apart and drive you forward. Let's review this again.

To identify your own superpowers, start by reflecting on your experiences, both personal and professional. Ask yourself these questions:

- What comes naturally to me?
- What do I excel at?
- What qualities do others admire in me?

But it's not just about your strengths—your values play a vital role, too. By aligning your career choices with your core values, you'll find a sense of purpose that fuels your leadership journey. Ask yourself:

- What is my North Star on issues such as honesty, teamwork, customer commitment, safety, and community involvement?
- Is my North Star focused on technical innovations, social causes, medical advancements, or environmental issues?

This is only a small list of examples for you to consider as you think about your personal values and motivations. Your company likely has a list of their core values, so you should review it to determine how they fit with your own values. If the two lists are aligned, career growth will likely come more easily for you than if you were with an organization whose values didn't match yours. And sometimes, understanding what's missing from the list of values is as important as what's included.

Your strengths and values are what will propel you to new heights. They'll help you navigate challenges, make tough decisions, and inspire others to follow your lead. Take the time to get to know yourself and let that self-awareness be the compass that guides you on your path to becoming a CEO.

As we discussed in Chapter 6, one of the best ways to determine your strengths and growth opportunities is by taking a leadership skills assessment. There are lots of testing tools out there, and their insights are invaluable. And although companies often provide (and usually require) these assessments, they typically don't offer them to employees until they reach a certain level within the organization. If your employer doesn't offer you these evaluations, there are plenty of leadership tests you can access independently. It will be well worth the money it will cost you to determine your leadership strengths and developmental opportunities.

And speaking of developmental opportunities, don't overlook them! Sometimes development doesn't look like an opportunity at first glance. Let's explore this a little more.

EXPLORE DIVERSE PATHS

The beauty of your leadership journey is that it can (and should!) be as diverse and multifaceted as you are. Laura Herring, the founder and former CEO of IMPACT Group and author of *No Fear Allowed,* is an amazing woman who never gave up as she built her company. On an episode of *Preparing for the Possibility,* she shared:

> "The most important thing you can do is believe you can do it . . . whatever it is. Don't second guess yourself." [39]

Exploring different career paths allows you to learn new things and grow in unexpected ways. By experiencing various industries, roles, and challenges, you'll develop a versatile skill set and a broad perspective that will serve you well as a leader. There is no "one size fits all" when it comes to finding successful career paths. Finding the right path for you is part of the adventure!

An analogy I like to make with women is that working for different companies is like trying on different brands of shoes. Although most shoes have some basic similarities, you'll never know which brand is right for you until you try it on. There are a myriad of shoe brands available, each with their own quirks and styles and fits. There's no one brand that fits everyone perfectly. The same is true for company cultures. Often, the executive management defines and embodies their organization's culture. Some of those cultures may be a natural fit for you. Others you may have to fit into, which can leave you feeling uncomfortable.

You'll be best positioned for success when you find the fit that's right for you in an organization where you're free to be yourself, where you don't feel like you have to work at fitting in, and where your values and the company's values are aligned. You may have to try on a couple organizations before you find the right one.

Even within a company, a new role is an opportunity to learn, push yourself out of your comfort zone, and discover new facets of your potential. Whether you're working in finance, marketing, operations, or any other field, each experience adds a unique layer to your leadership toolkit.

Study the roles in your organization that are the powerhouse assignments. Understand how others got those roles. When you're early in your career, there will be many roles that will be important to your career trajectory for becoming a CEO. Identify them and work with your mentor to get assignments in these roles. And tell the people who are involved in talent management about your aspirations. Be proactive in getting yourself considered for important roles.

Shellye Archambeau, the former CEO of MetricStream, had a lot of experience in sales early in her career. On an episode of *Preparing for the Possibility*, she said:

> "When people tell you 'No,' it doesn't mean no forever, it means something is not right now." [40]

Here's the takeaway: If you ask to be considered for a role and it doesn't happen the first time, don't quit trying. Ask why you didn't get the role, eliminate the problems, and try again. The next time might be a "Yes."

And this is the best part: You don't have to have it all figured out from the start. Your career path should and will evolve over time. The key is to stay open to opportunities, take risks, and embrace the twists and turns as they come. Don't be afraid to explore, pivot, and try new things. Every experience, whether it's a resounding success or a learning opportunity in disguise, is a stepping stone on your path to becoming a well-rounded, adaptable leader.

SMOOTH SAILING THROUGH CAREER SHIFTS

Now let's talk about the big shifts, the moments when your career takes a major turn and you find yourself navigating uncharted waters.

Maybe it's a job change, a promotion, a new company, or a leap into a whole new industry. Or maybe it's a shift in your personal life, like starting a family or moving to a new city or country. Or maybe it is both at the same time!

Speaking of moving, many CEOs often relocate for their roles, taking on assignments in multiple locations, either within the same company or across different organizations. It's very difficult to become a CEO in an organization with multiple locations—and particularly in a multinational corporation—if you've never relocated before. This was a huge mistake that I made. I spent my entire career in a corporate office. I didn't realize the important experiences I was missing. Relocating isn't easy, but it's an extremely positive credential for you to have in your portfolio of experiences.

Whatever the shift is that takes your career in another direction, one thing is certain: How you navigate it can make all the difference in your career journey.

The keys to smooth sailing through career shifts is agility, adaptability, and a whole lot of optimism.

AGILITY

Agility is the ability to adapt quickly to changes, assess what's the same and what's different in a new situation, and see it as an opportunity for growth.

If you view the change as a setback, it's OK to briefly grieve, but avoid holding grudges. Demonstrate to your organization that you can bounce back stronger than ever.

That's exactly what Kathy Mazzarella, the CEO of Graybar, did. In an interview for *Preparing for the Possibility*, she shared a story with me that's a great example of her demonstrating agility in her career.[41]

Kathy thought that she was in line for a major promotion that she ended up not getting; a male colleague of hers received the promotion instead, and she had to report to him.

Initially, she was devastated and angry. But then she sought advice from a mentor (in this case, her father), who encouraged her to "Buck up" and advised her that this a pivotal point in her career and that others will be watching to see how she handles it.

With this advice in hand, this future CEO first congratulated her peer for getting the promotion and made sure the organization saw her as a team player. Then, she took the driver's seat in her career by continuing to do whatever was needed to support the team and remaining receptive to other promotions that came her way over the next several years.

Fast-forward, the CEO resigned, and she became the organization's first female CEO. Years later, she learned that how she handled her disappointment, even when she'd felt passed over for the promotion, was a clear demonstration to the board that she had the strength and character needed to assume the CEO role.

The moral of this story is to never underestimate the power of agility; you never know when it might demonstrate your strength in the future.

ADAPTABILITY

I've mentioned adaptability several times already in this book, and I'm not finished yet. Career shifts are all about learning to thrive in new environments, new roles, and new challenges. Those who are open to change and willing to learn and grow along the way will inevitably have the most success.

For many years, I was friends with a retired gentleman who was a former CEO for several companies. In his post-career years, he had a wonderful and fulfilling life that many people admired. I would occasionally have lunch with him and always used this opportunity to learn from him. His advice to me was simple but has stuck with me ever since: Happiness and success can only come when you are adaptable and willing to accept change.

He served as a soldier in World War II before working—and

relocating—for several international companies, some of which he was not initially enthralled with. Most of the companies he was involved with did well, while others didn't, and he would have to take a step backward. But despite the constant change, he never became disillusioned. He learned how to adapt. And how did he stay adaptable? He always embraced change to its fullest

OPTIMISM

Career shifts can be scary, but they can also be incredibly exciting—if you approach them with the right attitude. Instead of focusing on the challenges, try to see the opportunities. Instead of mourning what you're leaving behind, focus on what you're moving toward.

One of my own principles is to never believe I'm a victim. When things happened that disrupted my ideal path, I had to make a conscious effort to remain optimistic and positive. A leader never sees themselves as a victim. They have had some occasional bad luck, but they were never a victim. When I found myself staring bad luck in the face and I began to think "Poor me," that was when I would tell myself, "Stop it!" and step back to see how I could make some lemonade out of these lemons. Remember, a successful leader understands that they have ultimate control over things and, in the end, never sees themselves as a victim.

Here's a story that I often tell about optimism. Once, there was a young boy who was so optimistic that his parents worried about how he would handle disappointment in "the real world." One year, they decided that they needed to help him prepare for the disappointments that life would throw at him, so they gave him a pile of manure as a gift. The boy, always the optimist, shouted, "I know there's a pony in there somewhere!" Optimism will take you far; every successful CEO has a vision of what can be. Don't confuse being optimistic with being unrealistic. You must always remain vigilant to understand the difference between the two.

In summary, smooth sailing through career shifts is all about perspective. It's about being agile in how you deal with new experiences and disappointments, being adaptable in how you learn and grow, and being optimistic in how you approach the future. It's about staying focused on your ultimate career vision and trusting that every shift, every challenge, and every opportunity is leading you closer to your goals. Remember what we discussed earlier: Luck follows those who are prepared.

So embrace the shifts. Lean into the challenges. And never lose sight of the amazing leader you're becoming along the way.

CHART YOUR DESTINATION

Let's talk about your career GPS. Just like any great journey, your career path needs a clear destination to guide you through the twists, turns, and unexpected detours.

Your career destination isn't just about a job title or a salary. It's about the impact you want to have, the legacy you want to leave, and the fulfillment you hope to find along the way. It's a vision that resonates with you and propels you forward, even—or especially—on the toughest days. So how do you define your career destination? What would your course look like if you had no fear?

I've stated this several times in past chapters, but it bears repeating. You need to get clear on the following big questions:

- What does success look like to me?

- What kind of leader do I aspire to be?
- What problems do I want to solve?
- What mark do I want to leave on the world?

Dig deep and dream big. Your career destination should reflect your authentic self—not what others or society say is the right path. You should pursue what truly matters to you, what sets your soul on fire, and what gives your work meaning and purpose.

Once you've got a clear vision of your destination, it's time to start charting your course. Break down your ambitious goal into smaller actionable steps. What skills do you need to develop? What experiences do you need to gain? What relationships do you need to build?

Your career destination isn't set in stone. As you learn and evolve, your vision may shift and change. That's a sign of growth. The key is to stay true to your core values, to your North Star—a guiding light that keeps you focused and on track, no matter what challenges come your way. So take the time to define it, refine it, and use it as you navigate your path to leadership.

TRANSFORM DIVERSIONS INTO PATHWAYS

Listen up, future CEO, because we're about to take a detour. But don't fret—this isn't a setback. It's an opportunity in disguise.

The path to leadership isn't linear. It's a winding road, full of unexpected twists, turns, forks, and diversions. While it's easy to view these detours as setbacks, the truth is they can be some of the most transformative moments of your career journey, equipping you for what's next.

Diversions are a natural part of any career journey. They're the moments when you're pushed out of your comfort zone, forced to adapt, and challenged to grow in ways you didn't expect. While they can be scary, they can also be incredibly rewarding . . . if you approach them with the right mindset. As Rhonda Hamm-Niebruegge, the executive director of St. Louis International Airport, stated in an episode of *Preparing for the Possibility*:

"There will be a learning curve. Don't be afraid of it." [42]

Start by reframing your perspective. Instead of seeing a detour as a roadblock, try to view it as a new route to your destination.

Ask yourself, "What can I learn from this experience? How can I use this challenge to develop new skills, gain new insights, or build new relationships?"

When you take the time to really analyze your "setback" or "detour," you'll almost always find that it can prepare you for what's next, even when you don't realize it at the time.

A CEO friend of mine believed he knew what the path to CEO was. His first roles—many in engineering and several roles in operations—all followed his plan. This was his dream, and it was becoming reality. Nothing unexpected on his path. But suddenly, his career trajectory took an unexpected turn when he was asked to work in government/public relations, leaving him feeling exiled and questioning what he had done wrong.

Instead of sulking, he followed his mentor's advice and embraced this new role as an opportunity to learn, excelling for a couple years in this new environment. He connected with people outside of his organization, and he came to better understand how our government works on a local, state, and national level. After a few years of proving he could handle this role, the organization moved him into a position that put him back on his "ideal" pathway to CEO. Years later, as CEO, he discovered that the experience he gained from that detour in government and public relations was critical to his success. Could he have ever imagined how important that role would become early in his career? Probably not. But he made the most of it and moved forward to learn as much as could. A valuable lesson for many of us.

I talked with Leslie Gill, the president and CEO of Rung for Women, about assuming roles that are outside your career path. She said:

> "Take the assignment. Take the project. Do it with an open mind and an open heart and always show up!"[43]

Remember, no two paths to CEO are identical. By taking control, setting your destination, and embracing the unexpected detours, you'll be well on your way to confident and resilient leadership. And you'll be more likely to choose a path that you'll enjoy along the way.

MANAGE YOUR CAREER

It's time to seize control of your career trajectory. No more allowing others to totally dictate your path or leaving your success to chance. Your career needs to reflect who you are, what you stand for, and the stamp you hope to make on the world.

It's your responsibility to steer it toward your dreams.

You must actively manage your career to reach your ultimate goals. You can't afford to be a passenger in the journey of your own professional life. You need to be the captain, navigating your course with intention and unwavering determination.

Impactful leaders who have achieved their career goals didn't get there totally by chance or luck. They took charge of their own development, learned from the detours, made strategic decisions regarding next steps, and never allowed others to define their ultimate success.

With intention, strategy, and a fierce determination, there's no limit to how far you can go.

Remember, your leadership journey is a winding path filled with challenges, triumphs, and unexpected detours. But with the right mindset, the right tools, and the right people by your side, there's no limit to how far you can go.

So step into your power, own your unique path, and let your leadership light shine bright. The world is waiting for a CEO like you.

ABC CALLOUTS

Let's recap the ABC's of how to plan your path to CEO:

A. **Align with your strengths, values, and aspirations:** Craft a path that follows these leads. Your leadership journey is unique to you. Use this as your North Star to guide your decisions and keep you motivated through challenges.

B. **Bold leaders embrace the twists and turns:** Let your experiences shape you into the well-rounded leader you can become. Exploring diverse career paths is a strength, not a weakness. And experiencing different companies with different cultures may be important to find what fits you. Every role, every industry, and every challenge is an opportunity to learn, grow, and expand your leadership toolkit.

C. **Captain your ship and take control of your career:** Set your course and steer toward your goals with purpose and determination. Don't let others dictate every turn in your path or define your career destination.

CEO
INSIGHT

"The question isn't who is going to let me; it's who is going to stop me."

—————

—Ayn Rand, author of *The Fountainhead*

Conclusion

PREPARE FOR THE POSSIBILITY NOW

BECOME THE LEADER YOU'RE MEANT TO BE

Congratulations, future CEO! You've now got a glimpse of this incredible journey and the reward at the end. It's a journey that takes you through the twists and turns of leadership, the triumphs and challenges of the climb to the top, and the endless possibilities that await you as you step into your full potential as a leader.

As we reflect on the path we've traveled together, a few key themes emerge—themes that will serve as your North Star as you navigate the uncharted waters of your own leadership journey.

First and foremost, remember that your path to becoming a CEO is uniquely your own. There is no one-size-fits-all formula for success, no predetermined route to the top. Your journey will be shaped by your own passions, strengths, and experiences—and that's precisely what will make you the kind of authentic, transformative leader the world needs. So embrace your unique leadership style!

Next, remember that the path to leadership isn't without its challenges—and that's where the importance of continuous learning, adaptability, and resilience comes in. As a CEO, you'll face countless obstacles and setbacks, from market disruptions to personal crises to societal upheavals. Your training begins now. The key is to approach your challenges with a growth mindset and a willingness to learn, evolve, take calculated risks, and develop a deep well of inner strength and resilience.

Finally, keep in mind that leadership is about more than achieving success for yourself—it's about making a positive impact on the world around you. As a CEO, you'll be able to shape your company's culture, respond to your customers' ever-changing needs with new products and services, and influence how other stakeholders view the value of the company's contribution to the larger global community. Your influence reaches far and wide.

So, as you step into this next chapter of your leadership journey, let these lessons be your guide. Embrace your unique path, and trust in the power of your own vision and abilities. Cultivate a deep commitment to continuous learning and growth, and approach every challenge with adaptability and resilience. And, most importantly, lead with purpose and integrity, knowing that your impact will ripple out far beyond the walls of your organization.

EMBRACE THE JOURNEY

Becoming a CEO isn't a destination—it's a journey. And like any great adventure, it's filled with mystery. You don't know how your story will unfold, how you'll break away from the pack, the failures you'll encounter, and the thrills you'll experience when you hit a home run. And in the end you may make a meaningful impact on the world around you.

As you navigate the path to leadership, remember that the journey is just as important as the destination. Even if you decide that becoming a CEO isn't the end goal for you, you'll be a better leader in so many ways if you incorporate the ideas this book provides. Every experience, every relationship, every challenge, and every opportunity are chances to learn and grow—to become not just a better leader but a better person. But my hope for you is that you make it to the CEO chair and that your influence will be felt far and wide.

So embrace the journey in all its messy, unpredictable glory. Be curious, be brave, get the right kind of experiences, and be willing to take risks and step outside your comfort zone. Surround yourself with people who challenge and inspire you, and never stop learning and growing.

Most importantly, remember that leadership is not about titles or accolades—it's about making a positive difference in other people's lives. It's about inspiring and empowering those around you to be their best selves and working together to create something greater than the sum of its parts.

So go forth, future CEO, and lead with courage, compassion, and conviction.

The corner office and the world are waiting for you!

"It always seems impossible until it's done."
—Nelson Mandela

READY TO TAKE
THE NEXT STEP?

Your journey doesn't end here—it's just beginning.

Access exclusive resources, join our growing community, and get the guidance you need to navigate your path to CEO.

From practical tools to mentorship and inspiration, *ABC to CEO* is here to support you every step of the way.

Scan the code or visit abctoceo.org

You have what it takes. Let's get you there.

ENDNOTES

[1] "Global CEO Gender Parity a Lifetime Away Despite Record Women CEO Appointments," Russell Reynolds, January 22, 2024, https://www.russellreynolds.com/en/about/newsroom/global-ceo-gender-parity-a-lifetime-away-despite-record-women-ceo-appointments.

[2] Billie Jean King, *Pressure Is a Privilege: Lessons I've Learned from Life and the Battle of the Sexes* (LifeTime Media, 2008).

[3] Luann Abrams, interview by Sharon Fiehler, *Preparing for the Possibility*, ABC to CEO, September 9, 2021, audio, https://www.abctoceo.org/luann-abrams#video.

[4] DeLisa Guerrier, interview by Sharon Fiehler, *Preparing for the Possibility*, ABC to CEO, January 25, 2024, audio, https://www.abctoceo.org/delisa-guerrier.

[5] Jenny Bristow, interview by Sharon Fiehler, *Preparing for the Possibility*, ABC to CEO, July 21, 2020, audio, https://www.abctoceo.org/jenny-bristow.

[6] Maryann Bruce, interview by Sharon Fiehler, *Preparing for the Possibility*, ABC to CEO, March 24, 2021, audio, https://www.abctoceo.org/maryann-bruce.

[7] Melinda French Gates, *The Moment of Lift: How Empowering Women Changes the World* (Flatiron Books, 2019), 2.

[8] Tracey Brophy Warson, interview by Sharon Fiehler, *Preparing for the Possibility*, ABC to CEO, September 4, 2020, audio, https://www.abctoceo.org/tracey-brophy-warson.

[9] Jocelyn Mangan, interview by Sharon Fiehler, *Preparing for the Possibility*, ABC to CEO, July 10, 2023, audio, https://www.abctoceo.org/jocelyn-mangan.

[10] Adrian Bracy, interview by Sharon Fiehler, *Preparing for the Possibility*, ABC to CEO, July 30, 2021, audio, https://www.abctoceo.org/adrian-bracy#video.

[11] Margo Cook, interview by Sharon Fiehler, *Preparing for the Possibility*, ABC to CEO, June 10, 2020, audio, https://www.abctoceo.org/margo-cook-1.

[12] Stacy Since, *Preparing for the Possibility*, ABC to CEO, November 3, 2022, audio, https://www.abctoceo.org/stacy-taubman.

[13] Noreen Doyle, interview by Sharon Fiehler, *Preparing for the Possibility*, ABC to CEO, November 19, 2020, audio, https://www.abctoceo.org/archive-women-in-finance.

[14] Daisy Dowling, *"Balancing Parenting and Work Stress: A Guide,"* Harvard Business Review, March 9, 2017, https://hbr.org/2017/03/balancing-parenting-and-work-stress-a-guide.

[15] Irl Engelhardt, email message to author, November 19, 2024.

[16] Mona Andrews, *Preparing for the Possibility*, March 1, 2024, audio, https://www.abctoceo.org/mona-andrews.

[17] Beth Chesterton, email message to author, January 15, 2025.

[18] Kathy Mazzarella, interview by Sharon Fiehler, *Preparing for the Possibility*, ABC to CEO, February 8, 2019, audio, https://www.abctoceo.org/kathy-mazzarella.

[19] Jenny Just, interview by Sharon Fiehler, *Preparing for the Possibility*, ABC to

CEO, May 17, 2023, audio, https://www.abctoceo.org/jenny-just.

[20] Lauren Herring, interview by Sharon Fiehler, *Preparing for the Possibility*, ABC to CEO, June 9, 2020, audio, https://www.abctoceo.org/lauren-herring.

[21] Jeane Hull, interview by Sharon Fiehler, *Preparing for the Possibility*, ABC to CEO, August 3, 2020, audio, https://www.abctoceo.org/jeane-hull.

[22] Jenny Johnson, interview by Sharon Fiehler, *Preparing for the Possibility*, ABC to CEO, January 26, 2021, audio, https://www.abctoceo.org/jenny-johnson.

[23] Bisa Grant, "Women in Engineering Panel," interview by Sharon Fiehler, *Preparing for the Possibility*, ABC to CEO, November 17, 2022, audio, https://www.abctoceo.org/women-in-engineering.

[24] Andra Kidd, interview by Sharon Fiehler, *Preparing for the Possibility*, ABC to CEO, December 14, 2023, audio, https://www.abctoceo.org/andra-kidd.

[25] Kim Popovitz, interview by Sharon Fiehler, October 16, 2024.

[26] Michael Altshuler (@michaelaltshuler1), "Let this be a reminder that we have the power to direct our lives and make the most out of the time we have," Instagram, December 19, 2023, https://www.instagram.com/p/C1CYYTYuOvg/?hl=en.

[27] Vanessa Fuhrmans, "A Decade After 'Lean In,' Progress for Women Isn't Trickling Down," *The Wall Street Journal*, September 17, 2024, https://www.wsj.com/lifestyle/careers/a-decade-after-lean-in-progress-for-women-isnt-trickling-down-f0e34074.

[28] Greg Boyce, interview by Sharon Fiehler, *Preparing for the Possibility*, ABC to CEO, September 8, 2020, audio, https://www.abctoceo.org/greg-boyce.

[29] Donna Brandin, interview by Sharon Fiehler, *Preparing for the Possibility*, ABC to CEO, November 19, 2020, audio, https://www.abctoceo.org/archive-women-in-finance.

[30] Laura D'Asaro, *Preparing for the Possibility*, ABC to CEO, September 14, 2022, audio, https://www.abctoceo.org/laura-dasaro#video.

belief and support in my vision gave me the confidence to pursue this project.

Irl Engelhardt and Greg Boyce: the two CEOs I had the privilege of working with, both of whom always had confidence in me. Your leadership and trust helped shape the course of my successful and fulfilling career, and for that, I am forever grateful.

My husband: Thank you for your patience, love, and support as I dedicated countless hours to writing this book. Your understanding made this possible, and now you have a partner again for all of the golfing, hiking, and biking that we love to do together. You will always be my "substance, sizzle and soul"!

And to my incredible team at Chapters:

Dan Curran, the cofounder of Chapters and my book manager, who believed in the mission of *ABC to CEO* from the moment he heard about it and always understood that sometimes life gets in the way of the schedule of writing a book. Without you, this book would have never become a reality.

John Ayers, the cofounder of Chapters, who saved me from many panic moments when I thought, "I lost everything!" and now understands that someone my age doesn't always get technology.

Lisa Caskey, my editor, who had the patience of a saint as I did revision after revision of my manuscript.

Jason Arias, my book designer, whose attentiveness and creative eye brought the vision of this book to life so beautifully.

Darnah Mercieca, my creative director and publishing strategist, who always knows what would appeal to others before even they know it.

ABOUT THE AUTHOR

Sharon Fiehler is the founder of ABC to CEO, a 501(c)3 organization dedicated to empowering young women to envision and achieve leadership roles, including the coveted position of CEO. Sharon believes that getting women into the C-suite is not enough and that we need more women prepared with the right experience to take on the role of CEO. With a mission to inspire one million young women to realize their leadership potential, Sharon's work focuses on providing the knowledge, strategies, and belief systems needed to navigate the complexities of career advancement into positions that will align young women with the experiences needed to be considered for a CEO.

Since the CEO position influences our society and serves our world, Sharon believes that having more women in the role of CEO will make our world a better place. ABC to CEO plants a seed at an early stage in the career of young women to imagine becoming a CEO, a role they may not otherwise imagine is within their reach, and then provides them with the knowledge to know what experience may take them there and what experiences will likely take them to a dead end.

Sharon also hosts the ABC to CEO podcast, *Preparing for the Possibility*, where she interviews CEOs and other senior leaders to share insights and advice for ambitious young women.

Sharon's expertise comes from a career as a former C-suite executive at a Fortune 500 company, where she managed global teams in IT, supply chain management, HR, and more. Sharon also chaired the 8th District of the Federal Reserve of the United States and, in 2007, was named one of Forbes's "15 Highest Paid Women in Corporate America."